D1604345

The Puritans on Conversion

Sin - The Greatest Evil
Samuel Bolton

The Conversion of a Sinner
Nathaniel Vincent

The One Thing Necessary
Thomas Watson

(Edited by Rev. Don Kistler)

Foreword by Albert N. Martin

Soli Deo Gloria Publications
..for instruction in righteousness...

Soli Deo Gloria Publications
P.O. Box 451, Morgan, PA 15064
(412) 221-1901/FAX 221-1902

*

These writings first appeared in the 17th century in
3 different books. This compilation is © 1990
by Soli Deo Gloria Publications and
Don Kistler. Printed in the USA.
All rights reserved.

*

ISBN 1-877611-11-5

TABLE OF CONTENTS

Editor's Preface

This collection of Puritan writings, comprised of two sermons and a treatise, begins what we hope will be a long series entitled, **The Puritans On_____**. The potential for a significant series is evident. Anyone who has read the rich writings of the Puritan Divines has been touched by their sense of reverence for God and His majesty, their awe at His beauty, and their recognition of His sovereignty. Who can spend time with these men without having their concept of God elevated to a higher plane? Who can read these masters of Scripture without realizing that we have lost the intimate knowledge of God they had?

With this volume we pay tribute to those who have gone before us in this work. In the 19th century, the work of James Nichols and James Sherman paved the way with their labors of love in seeing so many of the works of the Puritans revised, edited, and made available once again. In this century, Jay Green and his Sovereign Grace Trust, Iain Murray and the work of the Banner of Truth Trust, and Lloyd Sprinkle have enriched the Christian community with their reprinting of classic Puritan writings. Undoubtedly, there are many more of whom we are unaware, but we know that God is aware of them and will reward them accordingly!

The editing of these three works into one volume has not altered their content substantially. Paragraphs that ran for pages have been broken down into a more

Editor's Preface

readable format. Punctuation has been added or deleted to conform to more contemporary standards. Spelling has been changed where necessary, so that "easie." has become "easy." Words whose meanings have become obscure have been changed in the text to a more common usage, so that "cozen" has been changed to "deceive." This was done using the Oxford English Dictionary.

No theological alterations have been made, as we do not presume to think that we could better express the hearts of these men than they were able to do themselves. The Scripture verses have been left intact in whatever form was used in the original, punctuation and all. The only change has been to capitalize pronouns that refer to the Deity.

We trust, dear reader, that our efforts will be used of God to deepen your knowledge of Him, and thereby your love for Him. If such is the case, then the labor involved in editing and reproducing these writings will never be thought of as tedious or in vain. To that end, we commit this work to His Sovereign hand to use as He pleases.

To His Glory,

Don Kistler
Soli Deo Gloria Publications

FOREWORD TO
"THE PURITANS ON CONVERSION"

The most crucial issue with which the human mind and heart can ever grapple is that which is bound up with the question, "How can sinful man be made right with God?" All who have ever held to the Biblical and Apostolic faith have agreed that the only ground of the sinner's acceptance with God is comprised of the work of the God-man Christ Jesus Who, as the sin-bearing substitute of His people, procured a perfect righteousness as the fruit of His life, death, and resurrection (Rom. 5:19).

However, the Scriptures make it abundantly clear that none are brought into possession of this Christ-wrought righteousness except in the way of a thorough conversion to God (Acts 26:16-18, Matt.18:3). What is involved in true conversion is the area in which there is abounding confusion and frightening delusion in our day, even among the evangelicals who are clear on the question of the ground of the sinner's acceptance with God. It is precisely in the area of setting forth the Biblical doctrine of conversion that the Puritan preachers have so much to teach us.

While Joseph Alleine's book **ALARM TO THE UNCONVERTED**, and Richard Baxter's **CALL TO THE UNCONVERTED** have gone through numerous reprints in the past few decades, and have become

Foreword

a model of Puritan preaching on the doctrine of conversion, the three shorter treatises combined in this volume give us the heart of the same Puritan understanding of the doctrine of conversion.

The advantage of this trilogy is that each sermon has its own distinct areas of strength in setting forth both a sound theology of conversion as well as penetrating pastoral insights into the method of conversion. In contrast to much evangelical preaching and writing in our day, these three sermons are marked by the distinctive Puritan characteristics in the broad areas of the <u>content</u> of their doctrine of conversion, and in the <u>manner</u> in which they preached that doctrine.

THE CONTENT OF THEIR
DOCTRINE OF CONVERSION

1. They show the horrible evil of sin without in any way clouding the magnitude of the grace of God. Bolton's treatise is especially helpful in showing that one cannot overstate the horrible evil of sin. Further, Bolton's treatise, along with the other two messages, forever silences any just accusation that a preoccupation with the details and the extent of the evil of sin will cloud an appreciation of the magnitude of God's grace.

Foreword

2. The sermons demonstrate the necessity of a felt consciousness of sin without in any way constricting the freedom of the sinner's access to Christ or the duty of an immediate application to God for pardoning mercy.

3. Each of these sermons presses home to the conscience the absolute necessity of a deep and thorough repentance if there is to be any genuine faith in the promise of pardon to believing sinners. Unlike the "cheap grace" concepts in our day, these authors demonstrate, in convincing fashion, that Jesus Christ came to save His people from their sins, but not in them.

4. Each of these authors is clear with respect to the currently agitated question of whether or not Christ can be received as Savior while not being acknowledged as Lord. As an example of this assertion, Vincent demonstrates that in true conversion converts are turned from "the darkness of ignorance." Then he goes on to cite one of the specific areas in which this turning occurs. He writes, "They are made to know that Christ is to be received by faith, and that there is no salvation in any other, and that it is vain to expect anything from Him as a Saviour unless there is a consenting to obey Him as a Lord. These and like truths are no longer hidden from them." Later on in the same treatise he writes, "The convert eyes God as a lord. He owns His sovereignty and submits himself unto His

Foreword

scepter. *Other Lords indeed in times past have had dominion over him* (Isaiah 13), but now his resolution is fixed and peremptory to own no other Lord but God alone. His will stoops unto, and complies with, the will of God."

5. These treatises show a dominance of a God-centered view of conversion. While there is no veiling of the realities of the peace and joy which the penitent, believing sinner enjoys, there is a constant emphasis upon the fact that in conversion it is God's aim to bring the sinner back to the original intention for which he was created - namely, to a life of God-centeredness. Again, the words of Vincent are most perceptive when he writes, "The convert eyes God as his Ultimate End, that God may be glorifed, that God may be enjoyed in His design for turning. The sinner is sensible, while unconverted, that he lived to the dishonor of Him who gave him life, and in whose hand his breath is. Now therefore he has more zealous desires to walk worthy of the Lord unto all pleasing."

6. They constantly set forth the greatness and magnitude of the work of conversion, and its utter impossibility without a direct and sovereign intervention of God. One of the curses of our day is the widespread notion that salvation is "simple." While the essence of the message of God's salvation is indeed simple, to have the sinner thoroughly divorced from his sins, his own righteousness, and to give himself up

Foreword

to God on Gospel terms is a thing which our Lord Himself said is "impossible with men." These Puritan authors have captured the realism of that statement of our Lord, and are not afraid to set it forth in bold and convincing statements.

7. They show us that preaching the elementary truths concerning conversion must be done in a manner that is vigorously doctrinal and eminently Biblical. Wherever one turns in these three sermons, he will find Scripture illustrating and enforcing Scripture, and an evident grasp upon the balance of truth. In their most impassioned appeals to the consciences of their hearers, these authors never upset the delicate balance wheel of a sound systematic theology.

THE MANNER IN WHICH THEY PREACHED THE DOCTRINE OF CONVERSION

One cannot read these sermons without being struck with the dominant characteristics of the manner and method of the preaching of these men in contrast to the folksy, easy-going, casual, and non-confrontational preaching that marks much of current evangelicalism. I have noted only a few of the characteristics of the manner of their preaching which are worthy of emulation.

1. They are models of a kind of holy relentlessness

Foreword

and passionate tenacity in pressing their hearers to the one end that they might see them converted. One need only read "The Dedication" and "The Epistle to the Reader" at the beginning of Vincent's treatise to see that he is unashamed in committing himself to the great end of securing the conversion of his hearers. It is this holy passion which caused their sermons to be marked by pointed appeals to the conscience, specific applications with reference to sin, the struggles of the soul, the questions precipitated by doubt, and their boldness in addressing objections to an immediate and hearty compliance with their calls to conversion.

2. Their sermons are marked by a compelling chain of reason and argumentation. While these men believed firmly in the absolute spiritual deadness of the sinner, they did not believe that man had lost his capacity to feel the pressure of reasonable arguments. One marvels at their skill in driving people from the various "refuge of lies" in which they have sought to hide from the living God. Also, Scriptural reason and logic are brought to bear upon both the terrors connected with the state of impenitence and unbelief, and also upon the blessedness and desirability of being in a state of grace and acceptance with God.

3. It is evident that these men were not afraid of being labeled "excessive" in their passion. One said of the saintly McCheyne, who shared much of the spirit of the Puritans, that "he preached as if he were dying

to have men converted." This unashamed passion which throbs through the printed sermons of these men, leaping over centuries and changes of literary style, etc., is one of the most glaring deficiences of current evangelical and even of much reformed preaching. God Himself is unashamed to demonstrate passion when He expostulates with the words, "Turn ye, turn ye, for why will ye die?" So these men were unashamed to let the passion of genuine concern for the souls of their hearers be shown throughout their closely reasoned and eminently Biblical appeals.

For the reader who is unfamiliar with the standard Puritan authors, a first reading of the treatises in this book could give a wrong impression. One must remember that the Puritan views on justification by faith alone through the imputation of the righteousness of Christ was as clear as that of Martin Luther. This note is certainly sounded in these treatises. For example, Bolton writes, "Christ has left nothing for us to do, but to receive what He has purchased and laid up in the hands of the Father; nothing but sue out an acquittal, yes, and at the hands of Him who is just and will not deceive us; at the hands of Him who will certainly bestow whatever His Son has so dearly earned at His hands." Bolton goes on to write, "And oh! How should this make us advance Christ, admire Christ, prize Christ! What should endear our hearts more to Christ

Foreword

than this, that He has borne our sins, and so borne them as we shall never bear them, if we have an interest in Him!" However, for a fuller treatment of the Puritan doctrine of justification, one should read such works as Volume 5 of Owen, Volume 8 of Goodwin, and the appropriate sections in the works of Robert Traill.

When opening up such texts, says Romans 4:4-5, these men asserted the freeness and fullness of salvation grounded in the work of Christ. But when handling such texts as Luke 13:24, which command us to "strive to enter in by the narrow gate," they did not hold back from an unfettered opening up and applying of the obvious pressure of such texts.

If there is to be any hope that a true doctrine of conversion will once again be sounded forth in the power and passion of the Holy Spirit, it is most likely that the authors of these sermons and these pages will be our most helpful guides.

The publisher is to be commended for making these three treatises on conversion accessible to our needy generation.

Albert N. Martin, Pastor
Trinity Baptist Church
Montville, New Jersey

Sin: the Greatest Evil

(On II Samuel 24:10)

by Samuel Bolton, D.D.
Late Master of
Christ College, Cambridge

(First Published in 1657)

Sin: The Greatest Evil

*"...and now I beseech Thee, take away the iniquity of
Thy servant, for I have done very foolishly...."*

(II Samuel 24:10)

The occasion of these words was the hand of God
upon the children of Israel for David's sin of numbering the people. You read in verse 2 that *"David commanded Joab to go and number the people,"* and at
first, *"Joab dissuaded him."*

But you will say, "Was it not lawful to number the
people? Did Moses not do the same in the wilderness
as well as Joshua and Nehemiah?"

Yes, but Joab saw the pride of Davids's heart in it,
as appears by his answer in verse 3, *"and Joab said
unto the King, Now the Lord thy God add unto the
people how many soever they be, an hundredfold, but
why doth my Lord the King delight in this thing? Notwithstanding, the King's word prevailed against
Joab,"* though indeed to his trouble and Israel's cost.

Happy it had been for David and Israel, too, if the
work had not been done, but Joab went and the number
was brought in. There were *"eight hundred thousand
men that drew sword, and the men of Judah were five
hundred thousand."*

Well, but what was the fruit? What was the effect
of this?

Sin: The Greatest Evil

1. You read, *"David's heart smote him,"* verse 10. That is, his conscience accused him. If conscience is not a bridle, it will be a whip. If it is not a curb, it will be a scourge. If you will not hear the warnings, you shall feel the lashings of conscience. If it does not restrain from sin by admonition, it will put us to pain by contrition.

2. But that was not all. God would punish him for the sin. And you may read the sin in the punishment. He had gloried in the number and, therefore, God would lessen the number. Yet He puts it to his choice which of the three judgments he will take, whether it be the seven years famine, three months flight before his enemies, or three days pestilence. Every one was a sweeping scourge.

But mark David's behavior. God threatens judgment, and David goes and mourns for sin. David's "heart-smiting" and his prayer, though set before yet seem to be afterward, and an affect of the prophet's discovery of sin, as appears by the verse which follows our text, *"when David was up in the morning, the word of the Lord came unto Gad, David's seer."* You see it rendered as a reason why his heart smote him and why he prayed thus, because the prophet had been with him, had convinced him of his sin, and had denounced God's judgments against him, whereupon *"David's heart smote him,"* and he prays, *"take away the iniquity of Thy servant, for I have done very foolishly."*

Sin: The Greatest Evil

But here it may be demanded why, when God threatened judgment, should David go and pray for pardon of sin? Why did he not desire God rather to forbear his strokes, to avert and turn away His wrath rather than to merely beg pardon of sin? Or if he had desired this, yet why did he not beg the other as well as that, and join them together in the same petition?

Answer 1. To teach us in all the pressures and evils upon our outward man to turn our thoughts inward and lament sin.

Answer 2. Because he saw sin as the cause of judgment and therefore desired the removing of this that the other might also be withdrawn.

Answer 3. Because he knew the judgment could never be removed in mercy unless the sin was taken away. Every preservation is but a reservation. Every deliverance is in justice, not in mercy, if sin is not taken away.

Answer 4. He was more apprehensive of the dishonor of God by his sin than of any judgment that his sin brought upon him.

Answer 5. Or he sees in sin the greatest evil, and therefore seeks the redress of that rather than of any other evil, *"take away the iniquity of Thy servant."*

In the text you may observe two parts of prayer: (1) **Confession**, and (2) **Petition.**

1. Confession, with self-judging: *"for I have done*

Sin: The Greatest Evil

foolishly."

2. Petition: *"take away the iniquity of Thy servant,"* joined with faith.

Here you have (1) the petitioner, David, setting forth his relation, *"Thy servant,"* (2) the petitioned, God, (3) the petition itself, *"take away* (or pardon) *the iniquity of Thy servant."* The phrase seems to have respect to the scapegoat, a type of Christ which was to carry away the sins of the people into the wilderness, Lev.16:22, thereby signifying Christ's taking away of sin.

There is little difficulty in the words but what we may make a difficulty. Indeed, it would be a making of a difficulty to go about to expound that which is so plain, rather than an unfolding of them, if I should tell you of the several distinctions men make of sin, three words in the Hebrew. By one they will have to be meant original sin, by another infirmities, by the other your grosser sins. But upon examination, I find them used promiscuously, and therefore such distinctions of them have no bottom.

The letters of the words and the outward face of the text speak three doctrines:

1. That God's servants may commit sin, commit iniquity: *"the iniquity of Thy servant."*

2. Fresh sinnings must have fresh repentings. If you renew your sins, you must renew your sorrows.

3. There needs to be fresh pardon for fresh revolts:

Sin: The Greatest Evil

"take away." He does not say, "Assure me it is taken away," but "take away." But this will not be the subject of my discourse now.

That which I intend to speak to shall be the time and occasion of these words, which was when God's judgment was threatened against him.

1. Sin truly is, and God's people apprehend it to be, the greatest evil in the world.

He does not say, "Take away the plague," or "take away the judgment," but "take away this sin." He looked upon sin as the greatest evil.

2. When God threatens to punish sin, it is the best way to run unto God to take away sin. Or, when God's hand is either felt or feared, it should be a Christian's wisdom to repent of sin, to desire sin removed.

We begin with the first, that sin truly is, and God's people apprehend it to be, the greatest evil in the world. We will take it (1) in its pieces, and (2) we will close them. The doctrine divides itself into two parts: (1) that sin is the greatest evil in the world, and (2) that God's people apprehend it to be the greatest evil in the world.

For the first, that sin is the greatest evil in the world, I may show this (1) by collation and comparison of this with other evils, and (2) by demonstration and proof of it to you.

Sin: The Greatest Evil

If you compare the evil of sin with other evils, you shall see how short all other kinds of evils are to this evil of sin.

1. Most of all, other evils are only outward. They are only such as are on the body, the estate, the name, but this is an inward evil, an evil upon the soul, which is the greatest of evils.

2. All other evils are only of a temporal nature, they have an end. Poverty, sickness, disgrace, all these are great evils, but these, and all others, have an end. Death puts a conclusion to them all. But this evil of sin is of an eternal nature that shall never have an end. Eternity itself shall have no period to this.

3. All other evils do not make a man the subject of God's wrath and hatred. A man may have all other evils and yet be in the love of God. You may be poor and yet precious in God's esteem. You may be under all kinds of miseries and yet dear in God's thoughts. But now this is an evil that makes the soul the subject of God's wrath and hatred. The absence of all other goods, the presence of all created evils, will not make you hateful to God if sin is not there, so the presence of all other goods and the absence of all other evils will not render you lovely if sin is there.

4. All other evils only oppose your well-being, and your well-being for the present, for they cannot rob you of future happiness, but this opposes your well-being forever. You cannot be happy if you are not

Sin: The Greatest Evil

holy. Nay, this opposes your being. It brought you to death. You would sin yourselves into nothing again if God did not hold you up to be that you might be miserable for sin.

5. All other evils are only destructive to a man's self, they fight only against particulars. But this is contrary to the universal good being contrary to God, and is, as far as it may be, destructive to the very being of God, as I shall show hereafter.

6. All other evils are God's creatures, and so far good. He owns all the rest, He is the Author of all the rest. *"Is there any evil in the city that I have not done?"* (Amos 3:6), meaning all the evil of punishment penal, not sinful evil. But this is the Devil's creature, yea, and worse than he, being all sin.

7. All other evils are God's medicine and are used as medicines, either for the prevention of sin, or for the cure of sin.

For the prevention of sin: that you might not be condemned with the world, He lays afflictions and evils upon you, I Cor.11:32. He suffered Satan to tempt Paul, and gave him up to his buffetings, which yet is the greatest evil in the world next to sin, the greatest penal evil in the world. And all to prevent sin, as the Apostle himself said in II Cor.12:7, God sent a messenger of Satan to buffet him, and what was the reason? Why, it was to prevent sin lest he should be exalted above measure, that is, lest he should be proud.

Sin: The Greatest Evil

And as He uses all other evils for prevention, so for the cure of sin. You know no medicine can be as bad as is this disease. Now all other evils God has laid upon His people for the cure or for the recovery of them out of the state of sin. And to speak as much as I can at once, there is not as much evil in the damnation of a thousand worlds of men for sin as there is evil in the least sin, the least sinful thought that rises upon your spirits, inasmuch as the good of these falls short of the good and glory of God.

Thus you see, by collation and comparison of this evil with others in which I might more enlarge myself, that of all evils, sin is the greatest evil. We will now come to the demonstration of this point.

I. DEMONSTRATION

That which fights against and opposes the greatest Good must be the greatest evil, but now sin opposes and fights against the greatest Good. Hence a church father called sin "God-slaughter," that which strikes against the being and essence of God, that which, were it strong enough, were it infinitely evil as God is infinitely good, would labor to "un-be" God. God is *summum bonum*, and indeed, *non datur summum-malum*, sin cannot be infinite.

If sin were as evil as God is good, that is,

Sin: The Greatest Evil

adequately and proportionably, if infinitely evil as God is good, sin would be too hard for God to pardon. It would be too hard for God to subdue, too hard for God to conquer. Sin would endeavor to conquer God.

Indeed, there is more evil in the least sin than there is good in any, nay, all the angels of heaven. Therefore you see it conquered them, spoiled all their goodness, made them devils, which it could not have done if the good in them had been greater than the evil in sin.

And though it is not able to conquer God, to overcome Him (there is more goodness in God than evil in ten thousand hells of sin, and so it cannot overcome the power of God, the mercy of God, the holiness of God), yet it fights against God, and makes parley against Him every day. It musters up all its strength against God and comes into open field to bid defiance against Him every day.

Nay, when it is beaten out of the open field by the power of God and His ordinances, then it has strongholds, as the Apostle tells us in II Cor.10:4, and from thence fights against Him and opposes Him. There it lusts against Him, it wills against Him, the heart rises against Him.

When sin is beaten out of the field, yet a long time it will be before it is beaten out of the strongholds. When sin in practice is overcome and conquered, yet sin in affection is hard to be overcome. That con-

Sin: The Greatest Evil

trarity that is between God and your heart is hard to be conquered. It will cost you many a battle, many an assault, before you can conquer sin in its strongholds, overcome sin in the heart.

Though sometimes it may seem to be overcome and to render up all, yet afterwards it gathers together again and will make new and fresh assaults upon you, to weaken and wound you.

Nay, and herein lies the malignity, the poisonous and venomous nature of sin, that, though God has conquered it, though it is never so weakened, yet it will act against God and spit its venom still.

You have an emblem of it in the thief upon the cross. When he was nailed upon the cross, his hands and feet made fast and only one member loose, yet that one member could spit its venom at Christ, revile Christ. So though God has crucified sin, yet as long as there is any life in it, it will act itself and spit venom against God, which shows that great contrary between God and sin. And this contrarity and opposition of the chief good must show sin to be the greatest evil.

2. DEMONSTRATION

That which is univerally evil, all evil and no good, must be the greatest evil in the world. But sin is all evil. As we may say of God, "there is no evil in Him, He is

Sin: The Greatest Evil

good," so I may say of sin, there is no good in it, it is all evil!

There is some good in the worst things in the world, and something in the worst things to make them capable of our choice of them in some cases; some good in sickness, some good in death. But now there is no good in sin, nor can any considerations in the world make sin the object of our choice. Though you might avoid death by sin, yet sin is universally evil and no good in it, you may not make use of sin to avoid death.

And therefore you shall read that when the Apostle would speak the worst of sin, he could find no name worse than its own to set it out, Rom.7:13, *"sinful sin."* He calls it sinful sin, nothing but sin!

3. DEMONSTRATION

That which is the sole object of God's hatred must be the greatest evil. But sin is the sole object, not only the object, but the sole object of God's hatred. He hates nothing but sin. His love runs in divers streams toward all the things He has made, but His hatred runs in one channel alone, and that is toward sin.

If man were made the center of all other evils in the world, God could love him under all if sin were not there. And if there is a confluence of all other goods,

Sin: The Greatest Evil

health, beauty, riches, learning and so on, God hates
you if sin alone is there. God's love cannot be there,
but His wrath abides there.

4. DEMONSTRATION

That which separates the soul from the chief Good,
that which divides between the soul and God, the chief
Good, must be the greatest evil. But sin divides between God and the soul, Is.59:2, *"your iniquities have
separated betwixt you and your God,"* between your
souls and His grace, your souls and His comfort, your
souls and His blessings.

It was said of Naaman that he was a great man, an
honorable man, a mighty man of war, but he was a
leper, II Kings 5:1. So whatever ornaments a man has,
whatever gifts, parts, riches, beauty, etc., yet if he is a
leper, though a learned man, a rich man, if he is a
wicked man, that spoils all the rest.

5. DEMONSTRATION

That which is the ground and cause of all other
evils must be the greatest evil, but sin is the cause of
all other evils. Is the old world drowned with water? It
is for sin. Is Sodom destroyed with fire and turned

Sin: The Greatest Evil

into an asphalt lake to this day? It is for sin. Is Jerusalem laid on heaps? Sin has done it. Should I center on this I should find no end.

Sin is the cause of all national evils. We will name some and only name them.

1. Wars-

Judges 5:8 *"They chose new gods, then there was war in the gates."*

James 4:1 *"From whence come wars and fightings among you? Is it not from your lusts?"*

2. Famine-

Ps.107:34 *"He turneth a fruitful land into a desert for the wickedness of them that dwell therein."*

Amos 4:6 *"Therefore* (for their sins) *have I given you cleanness of teeth in all your cities, and scarceness of bread in all your places, etc."*

3. Pestilence- Note David's sin of numbering the people in Deut.28:21, *"The Lord shall make the pestilence to cleave to thee, till He hath consumed thee*

Sin: The Greatest Evil

from off the land, whither thou goest to possess it."
And as sin is the cause of national evils, so of personal
evils, and those are (1) temporal, (2) spiritual, and (3)
eternal.

Sin is the cause, the meriting, the procuring cause
of all. All evils are but the births of sin. Sin is a big-
bellied evil and all other evils are but the births of sin.
Those upon your bodies: sickness, aches, pains, weak-
nesses. Those upon your souls: fears, heart-breakings,
terrors, horrors. If you could rip up sin, you would find
all these to lie in the bowels of the least sin.

Shall I tell you? Sin was the first founder of hell,
that which laid the cornerstone of that dark vault, for
before sin there was no hell. No, and it was sin that
built up hell and has fitted hell with those treasures and
riches of wrath, fire, and brimstone. No, and that
which still adds to it and increases the fuel, Rom.2:5.
It treasures up wrath against the day of wrath.

Therefore, being a universal evil, a catholic evil,
the womb of evils and cause of all, it must be the
greatest evil.

6. DEMONSTRATION

That which is worse than the utmost evil must be
the greatest evil, but sin is worse than the utmost evil.
That which is greater than the greatest evil must be

Sin: The Greatest Evil

exceedingly great. Hell is the utmost evil, but sin is a worse evil than hell itself. Hell separate from sin is only miserable, not sinful; a penal evil, not a sinful evil.

Separate hell from sin (though we cannot really separate hell from sin, yet we may make an intellectual separation, we may abstract hell from sin in our understandings), and then I say sin is worse than hell because hell is only a penal evil, sin is a sinful evil. And there is no penal evil as bad as a sinful evil. There is good in the punishment, the good of justice, but no good in sin, and therefore sin in itself is the greatest evil.

Now we come to the second point, which is the main one. As sin is in itself, so in the apprehensions of God's people, sin is the greatest evil. Their sighs for sin, and their sufferings to avoid sin, show that they apprehend sin as the greatest evil.

1. Their sighs for sin— you may look into David's penitential Psalms and see what sighs and groans he had for sin. Look into Psalm 51. Why, what was the reason for them? All the sufferings, all the evils in the world, would not have affected him as much as his sin. Paul said, Rom.7:24, *"Oh wretched man that I am! Who shall deliver me from this body of death!"* The death of his body was nothing to him in comparison to this body of death!

Paul went through many tribulations, endured a

Sin: The Greatest Evil

great deal of sufferings, as you may read in II Cor. 11:23-25, yet all these scourges, these prisons and persecutions, did not go as much to his heart as sin, even the presence, though not the power of sin. Though he suffered much, yet we do not read that he ever cried for all of that. Yet he does cry for sin, "Oh miserable man that I am! Who shall deliver me from this body of sin!" So did Peter, Manasseh, etc.

2. Their sufferings to avoid sin— Daniel was content to be thrown into the den of lions, the three children into the fire, Paul and Silas into the stocks. And many of God's children have chosen to embrace prisons, stakes, fire, and the hottest persecutions rather than sin, which plainly evidences to us that they esteemed sin to be the greatest evil.

They esteemed it greater than poverty, which is a great evil. "Better to beg," said one, "than to sin." Heb.11:24-28, *"Moses chose to rather to suffer affliction with the people of God than to enjoy the pleasures of sin for a season."* One who was like Moses, Caleacius Caracciolus, was a noble prince and marquess who, that he might not sin, left and forsook all he had and took himself to live meanly with the people of God, merely to enjoy the ordinances.

Musculus, a man of excellent learning and a famous Divine, rather than sin, would close with any condition. The story tells us that, being driven out of all he had, he was content, rather than sin, to take

Sin: The Greatest Evil

himself to a poor trade, to be a weaver, to get bread to maintain his wife and children. Afterwards, being cast out of the way, the world looking upon itself as too good for him, he took himself to work with a spade in the common ditch of the town to get his living. He could be in any condition rather than sin.

They have not only apprehended sin to be a greater evil than poverty, but greater than death itself. It was the speech of Ambrose, "Will you cast me into prison? Will you take away my life? All this is desirable to me, rather than to sin."

When Eudoxia, the Empress, threatened Chrysostom, whom she afterward banished, he sent this message to her, "Go tell her," he said, "I fear nothing in the world but sin."

3. They have apprehended sin to be a greater evil than death. Basil speaks of a rich virgin who, being condemned to the fire and sentenced to lose her estate because she would not worship idols, yet afterwards was promised life and restitution of estate if she would. She replied, "Farewell life, let money perish." Look through the Ten Bloody Persecutions and our late Marian Days and you shall find many instances to this purpose.

4. Further, they have not only apprehended sin to be a greater evil than death, but more, a greater evil than hell itself. It was the speech of Chrysostom, "I thus think, and thus will I ever preach, that it is more

Sin: The Greatest Evil

bitter to sin against Christ than to suffer the torments of hell."

Anselm said that if on the one side were presented to him the evils of sin, and on the other side the torments of hell, he would rather choose to fall into hell than to fall into sin. At such a distance were their hearts from sin. And nothing is more ordinary than expressions such as these from the saints, in temptations, in troubles of spirit, or in clearing their own hearts: "Rather slay me, rather damn me, rather cast me into hell, than let me sin against Thee!"

But this shall be sufficient to clear the doctrinal part. We now come to the application.

1. CONSEQUENCE

If sin is the greatest evil in the world, then let us fall down and admire the wisdom and adore the goodness of God who, out of the greatest evil, could bring the greatest good; who makes the greatest evil an occasion of the greatest good that ever was wrought. Bernard was so taken up with the thoughts of it that he said, "Happy fault, which occasioned such a Redeemer!"

We should be humbled for the fault and bless God for the Remedy, and withal admire that wisdom and goodness which has taken occasion by man's wickedness to declare His own goodness; by man's sin to make known and express the infiniteness of His wisdom, power, mercy, justice, etc. That this should be an occasion to draw out all His glorious attributes; that He should bring good out of evil, life out of death, heaven out of hell, good out of sin, cordials out of poison.

Let us never doubt, never suspect, but that God can bring good out of anything, turn the greatest evils to the advancement of His glory and the good of His people; who can, out of sin and hell, bring good. What is it to turn afflictions, persecutions, the plots and malice of men? What is it to turn troubles, wars, etc., to His own glory, and the advancement of His cause, who was able to turn sin to all this?

He that can turn the evil of sin, which is pure evil and the greatest evil, can much more turn the evil of trouble to the good of His people. This made the Apostle say that all things should work together for them that love God. He that has experience of this needs not doubt anything else. That God who can turn sin can turn afflictions, crosses, persecutions and so on to the good of His church and His people.

2. CONSEQUENCE

Hence conclude, then, that it is the saddest punish-

Sin: The Greatest Evil

ment, the most fearful judgment in the world, to be given up to sin. This is the utmost punishment that God inflicts upon men and, therefore, the greatest of all punishments.

God usually proceeds by degrees in the way of His judgments. First, He begins with lesser. If lesser will not do, then He proceeds to greater. He will punish yet seven times more, and still the further He goes, the greater are His strokes.

Now this is the finishing, the concluding stroke, this is the last punishment and the greatest of all others, to give a man up to the state of sin; to say to a man, "You that are filthy, be filthy still, and you that are unclean, be unclean still." This He tells them in Ezek. 24:13, *"Because I would have washed thee, purged thee, and thou wouldst not be purged, therefore thou shalt not be purged."* And so He tells the Israelites, *"Because you would have altars to sin, therefore altars shall be to you to sin,"* Hosea 8:11.

Oh! There is no sadder judgment in the world than for a man to be given up to his own heart's lust. This sets an eternal night of darkness.

"Good Lord, deliver me from myself," said Augustine. You had better be given up to the lusts of men, to the malice and cruelties of bloodthirsty men; better to be given up to the utmost rage and malice of our bloody Irish rebels than to be delivered up to yourselves, to the lusts of your own hearts. Nay, you had

Sin: The Greatest Evil

better to be given up to Satan than to be given up to yourselves, your sins.

The incestuous person was delivered up to Satan, as you read in I Cor.5:5, and was restored again and the better for it. But we never read of any who were delivered over to themselves who ever returned, never any who were given up to the lusts of their own heart that ever recovered. Better, then, to be delivered up to Satan than to sin, inasmuch as all penal evils fall short of sinful evils.

It is judicial in respect of God who may punish one sin with another and curse sin with hardness of heart. But this is a sinful evil in respect of us. We bring the writing and the wax and God puts the seal on, and then we are shut up forever. And you are in the highway to this who go on in sin and will not be reformed. When God labored by sickness and afflictions to recover you, you are in the way to this final doom, *"You that are filthy, be filthy still!"*

3. CONSEQUENCE

If sin is greatest evil in the world, then see what fools they are who seek to rid themselves of other evils by the admission of sin. He who labors to prevent other evils, or remove other evils by the admission of sin, runs into the greatest evil of all. He kills himself to save himself. He destroys himself to preserve himself. He that thus saves his life loses his life.

There were never any times so bad but God's people might have been safe in them if they would have admitted sin. But they have seen their safety to lie in suffering when they could have no safety but in the admission of sin. You see it in the practice of the three children: Shadrach, Meshach, and Abednego.

It was the speech of the primitive Christians when they were threatened with prisons and death if they would not renounce Christ, "Good Emperor, you threaten a prison, but Christ hell!"

When Cyprian was sentenced to die upon the same grounds, the governor tried to reason with him that he should pity himself and renounce his error rather than lose his life. Cyprian answered him, "Sir, you are my judge, you are not my counselor. In so clear and just a cause there is no need of counsel. I will not dishonor the justness of my cause to enter into parley and consultation as to whether to suffer or sin." It is like the case of the virgin of whom Basil speaks, who bade adieu to estate and life rather than abandon her profession.

Oh! It would be a sad thing to secure ourselves by that which is our ruin, to purchase our liberty by bondage, our safety by sin. You see what it cost Frances Spira and Cranmer in Queen Mary's days, who knew not how to be avenged on himself for his act but by burning that hand first that had subscribed to sin.

It is better to be still in prison than for sin to set open the prison door, inasmuch as it is better to be God's prisoner than the devil's free man. Better to lose all than to preserve our estates by the admission of sin.

And therefore, whatever your troubles are, whatever your fears, whatever your dangers, beware of preserving yourselves or purchasing liberty or life itself at so dear a rate as by the admission of sin, by dishonoring God and wounding your own conscience. Beware of getting man as your friend by purchasing God to be your enemy.

We know not yet what our times may come unto, but it is out of the reach of the power or malice of men to make you miserable if they do not first make you sinful.

4. CONSEQUENCE

If sin separately considered is so great an evil, what, then, is sin circumstantiated? Sin against knowledge, against means? If there is so much evil in sin, in the least sin, what, then, in the greatest? If atoms are so great, how great, then, are mountains? If impertinent thoughts are so sinful, having more sin in them than all the treasures of heaven (besides God and Christ) can expiate, what, then, are rebellious thoughts, contrived murders, speculative adulteries, contemplative wickedness, covetous aims and ends, contempts of God, slightings and undervaluings of His ways? If there is so much sin and hell in a vain, idle word, what a hell of sin, what mountains of wrath are there in your carrion communications, your stinking discourses, your blood and horrid oaths and blasphemies?

Nay, if there is so much evil in one sin, and one sin simply considered, what shall we think of sin compounded, sin circumstantiated, sin made exceedingly sinful? Sins against knowledge? Against means? Against mercies? Oh! Sit down and consider one sin and see much in it. "Such a sin I committed against knowledge, such a one against checks of conscience, such a one against the motions of the Spirit, etc." And tell me if the least sin is not exceedingly sinful.

5. CONSEQUENCE

If sin is so great an evil, then see what fools they are who mock at sin, Prov.14:9, *"Fools make a mock at sin,"* they sport at sin. It is a sport to swear, to be drunk, etc. They will sin for sport and recreation. It is their recreation to do evil, to drink, to swear, to lie, to profane God's day. These are fools. What, natural fools? No. He that goes about with a whistle, a babble,

Sin: The Greatest Evil

and a coat is in a far better case. This one is a spiritual fool, the greatest fool.

Will you sport with poison? Will you sport yourselves with hell? Nay, worse! Will you recreate yourselves with destroying yourselves? Will you sport yourselves with that which was so bitter to Christ, and will be so to you if ever you are pardoned?

Who would sport at that which is the misery of lost men and devils, both here and in hell to eternity?

One would think this poor sport and recreation to tear in pieces the flesh, and wound and shed the blood of a stranger, of an enemy, but how much more of our dearest Friend? You who sport at sin do so with Christ. You sport in killing Christ, crucifying Christ, tearing the flesh of Christ again. Every oath is a dagger to His heart, as the spear to His side again.

It is the highest piece of a devilish nature in the world to sport at sin. None but devils do it . It is the burden of God. He complains of it and He accounts it an ease when He is rid of you, *"Ah, I will ease Me of My adversaries,"* Is.1:24.

It is the wounding of Christ, the grief of the Spirit, the trouble of angels, the destruction of creatures. Will you sport at that which has brought all evil on man, even on Christ? Which has made hell, fueled hell, and has been the torment of souls forever?

Oh! Make not that your joy which was Christ's sorrow, and will be yours eternally if your joy in sin is not turned to sorrow for sin.

6. CONSEQUENCE

If sin is the greatest evil, then see the utter impossibility of anything under heaven to relieve and help us from under the guilt of sin save Jesus Christ alone. Have you committed but one sin? You have done that which all the treasures of righteousness in heaven and earth are not able to relieve or help you in save **JESUS CHRIST**. There is as much required for the answering of the guilt of one sin as the guilt of a thousand. Infinite righteousness is required for one, and no more is required for a thousand. And that righteousness, none but Christ alone has.

Nothing can relieve us but that which is adequate in righteousness to the evil of sin. Now there is no righteousness in the world that is proportionable to the evil of sin but the righteousness of Christ. Our own, you know is too short, it is called a menstruous rag, Is.64:6. A rag, and therefore cannot cover us; menstruous and, therefore, though it should cover us, yet it would only cover filth with filth, as the prophet speaks in Isaiah 30:1, *"They cover, but not with the covering of My Spirit, that they might add sin to sin,"* that is, they add the sin of their righteousness to the sin of their unrighteousness. They cover a blot with a blot,

Sin: The Greatest Evil

they add sin to sin, dung to dung.

Nor will the righteousness of the Law be large enough, if it were supposed that a man were able to fulfill all that righteousness and keep the whole Law. Present obedience, though supposed to be adequate to the righteousness of the Law, will never answer for former offences and disobedience.

The Law is strong enough to damn a thousand, but cannot save one. It can pour hell, wrath, and condemnation upon a world of sinners, but is unable to pour grace, or to give justification to one. The Apostle tells us, Rom.8:3-4, *"What the Law could not do, in that it was weak through the flesh: God (sending His own Son, in the likeness of sinful flesh, and for sin) condemned sin in the flesh."* The same Apostle also tells us, Gal.3:21, *"If there had been a Law given which could have given life, righteousness should have been by the Law."* The Apostle tells us again, Gal.3:17, *"The law was given four hundred and thirty years after the promise,"* to show that we must not work that we may be justified, but be justified that we may be able to work. If God had intended the Law as the instrument of justification, He would not have given the Law four hundred and thirty years after the promise.

Nay, yet further, it is not the righteousness of angels (which yet is a greater righteousness than that of the Law inasmuch as the angels were above man in

Sin: The Greatest Evil

innocency) because this also is but a created righteousness, a finite righteousness, and no way proportionable to the evil of sin. If it had been, one sin would not have spoiled those glorious angels of their goodness at once and made them devils, which that sin did, showing that there was more evil in sin than good or righteousness in them.

Well, then, this shows the utter impossibility of any other under heaven or in heaven to free us from the evil of sin but **JESUS CHRIST**. Nothing but infiniteness can deal with sin. It must be infinite wisdom - to find a way. It must be infinite mercy - to pardon; infinite power - to subdue; infinite merit - to purge and cleanse; and infinite grace - to destroy sin.

However you think of sin, yet this has been the great enemy which God and grace have been contending with ever since the world began. And it has put All-God to it, even the infiniteness of the infinite God to rescue us, to save us out of the hands and power of sin. His infinite wisdom, power, mercy, truth, and holiness have all been employed to conquer sin; I say, so to conquer sin as to save you sinners.

The great design of God in sending Christ into the world, His incarnation, humiliation, death, and passion, were all about this: the conquering and destroying of sin. How great an enemy was this that God must send out His Son to conquer it? He can arm flies, lice, frogs, the meanest of creatures, to overthrow the greatest power and force on the earth, but no less than His Son was strong enough to conquer sin.

You may think of sin as meanly as you will, swallow it without fear, live in it without sense, commit it without remorse, yet assure yourselves that this you make so slight of required no less than the infinite power of God to conquer, the infinite mercy of God to pardon, the infinite merit of Christ to answer for it. It was that which fetched the dearest blood from the heart of Christ, and will have yours, too, if you do not get an interest in Him.

7. CONSEQUENCE

If sin is the greatest evil, then see how much we are bound to Christ, who has borne your sins, who has borne all this evil for you who have an interest in Him.

Oh, the love of Christ! That He should bear sin, which is more than all miseries, a greater evil than death, than hell itself!

If there were one in the world that was content to be poor for you, to bear pains for you, to be sick for you, to be arrested for you, to go to prison for you, to die for you, nay, to bear the wrath of God for you, nay, the pains of hell for you, how bound would you think yourselves to such a one for doing this?

Why, Christ has done this for you. He has borne

Sin: The Greatest Evil

sin, which is a greater evil than all of these, an evil that has all these evils in the bowels of it, such as none but Christ was able to bear.

If God has laid the least sin upon you, pure sin (which none but Christ ever bore here in the world), it would crush you to pieces with the weight of it though all the pillars of heaven and all the glorious angels should contribute their strength to help you to bear it up.

The least sin deserves and draws down an infinite wrath which neither you, nor all the angels in heaven, are able to stand under. The damned bear it in hell. They bear it and cannot bear it. They are slain with it but cannot die. Ever consuming, never consumed. And therefore, how much are you bound to **CHRIST**! who has borne sin, a greater evil than all other evils, and with sin, all the torments, wrath, and justice due to sin.

All the world is not able to express that torment which Christ endured when He bore sin, when He sweat drops of blood, clots of blood, when He wrestled with the justice and bore the wrath of God; when He cried out, *"My God! My God! Why hast Thou forsaken Me?"* A strange speech from Him who was the Son of God, which made the fathers of the Greek Church say, "By virtue of Thy unknown labors, and those sufferings not revealed to man, have mercy on us." It is no dishonor to say that whatever the sufferings of the

Sin: The Greatest Evil

the damned were, Christ endured, though not in kind. And therefore let me say again, how much are you bound to Christ who has borne your sins for you! And the more bound because it was a voluntary act of Christ, none could enforce or constrain Him to do it. Now the more willingly a courtesy is done, the better it is. This enhances and heightens a courtesy when it is done willingly.

We used to say of such good turns which come willingly that we account them double courtesies. The will makes all great as the more evil there is in sin, the greater is the sin. This applies to the sin against the Holy Ghost. It is done with devilishness and desperateness of will.

The more will there is in service, the more acceptable that service is. Whatever you do for God, the more will there is in it, the more God esteems it. The more will there was in this great act of Christ, the more are we bound to Christ for it.

Now if you look upon it from the beginning to the end, you shall find nothing but mere love, mere good will in it. His first undertaking of it was voluntary. It was a voluntary agreement between God and Christ, a willing contract made in heaven with God, that He would undertake this great work. And He came into the world with as much willingness, Heb.10:5-7, *"Wherefore, when He comes into the world, He saith, Sacrifices and offerings Thou would not have. In*

Sin: The Greatest Evil

burnt offerings and sacrifices for sin Thou hast no pleasure. Then said I, Lo, I come to do Thy will, O God," setting forth the freeness and willingness of Christ to undertake this work.

And hence the angels sang at His incarnation, "Good will to men." It was nothing but mere good will. And when He was in the world He carried on the work with as much good will. He tells us, *"for this end was I born, and for this end came I into the world,"* nay, and He said He was in pain until the hour came, viz. in pain of love until the hour came.

And when the hour came, though it was a black and dismal hour, called "The Hour of Darkness," yet He would not desert us, He would not leave us. If He had, He would have left us in hell without any recovery. But He would go through with it, though it made Him (as far as He was man) strange at the work of His mercy. Nay, He would bear sin and bear wrath and lay down the utmost drop of blood in His body.

Oh! Oh! Think with yourselves, you that are the people of God, how much you are bound to Christ!

How may we say with Bernard, "Thou art my life, I am Thy death. Thou my righteousness, I Thy sin. Thou my heaven, I Thy hell. Thou my riches, I Thy poverty." Oh, how are you bound to Christ, who has borne sin!

But yet more, how are you bound to Christ who has so borne sin as we shall not bear it, so paid the debt

Sin: The Greatest Evil

that we are discharged? Col.2:14, *"Blotting out the handwriting of ordinances that was against us and contrary to us, taking it away, and nailing it to His cross."* As the death of Christ was our payment, so the resurrection of Christ is our discharge, Rom.4:25, *"who was delivered for our offences, and rose again for our justification."* Are we not justified by His blood? Yes, we are, and therefore He did not rise formally to justify us, but to declare that we were justified, that we were acquitted, that our sins were pardoned.

Had Christ been still in prison under the chains of death, we could not have had any assurance that our debt had been discharged. As the Apostle says elsewhere, *"If Christ be not risen, we are yet in our sins."* But now Christ, being arrested, cast into prison, laid in the grave, and having broken the bands of death in which it was not possible for Him to be held, having risen again, by this is declared that our sins are discharged.

If indeed Christ had so borne sin as that yet we should bear it, what were we the better? But Christ having so borne sin as that we shall not bear it, how infinitely are we bound to Christ for this!

Christ has left nothing for us to do but to receive what He has purchased and laid up in the hands of a Father; nothing but sue out an acquittal, yes, and at the hands of Him who is just and will not deceive us; at the hands of Him who will certainly bestow whatever His Son has so dearly earned at His hands.

If a man dies and leaves legacies in the hands of such who are faithful, may we not go and require them? When Christ died, He entrusted all His merits into the hands of His Father, and He has left nothing for us to do but go and require all.

God entered into bond and covenant with Christ that, if He would bear sin, we should not bear them; that if He would die for sin, He would pardon sin, for all that is included in Is.53, *"He shall see the travail of His soul and shall be satisfied."*

Well now, Christ has done this, and, having done it, He has given all His Father's bills and bonds into our hands, and with all a letter of attorney whereby we are enabled to call for all this at the hands of God.

It was for us that Christ undertook the work, and all that Christ did was to engage God to us, first to satisfy Him, and then to engage Him, to make God our debtor who were His debtors. And as long as there is any of the blood of Christ to give out (which will never be spent, it is an everlasting righteousness), so long is the mercy of God, nay, the justice of God engaged to bestow it upon us who by faith come over to Him. And there remains nothing for us to do, in point of justification, but to sue out all the Christ has purchased.

We live in the world as if we were to purchase a pardon, when we are only to receive a pardon. God arrests us for the debt of sin, but do you think it is that we should pay it? Alas, poor creatures, no! It is but to drive us out of ourselves and to bring us over to Christ who has already paid the debt.

And oh! How this should make us advance Christ, admire Christ, prize Christ! What should endear our hearts more to Christ than this, that He has borne our sins, and so borne them as we shall never bear them if we have an interest in Him!

8. CONSEQUENCE

If sin is the greatest evil, then it calls out:

1. for the greatest sorrow
2. for the greatest hatred
3. for the greatest care to avoid it
4. for the greatest care to get rid of it.

If sin is the greatest evil, then it must have the greatest sorrow. No affliction, no trouble, no evil should be so bitter to us as sin, because sin is the greatest evil. It is a sad thing to see our hearts tender and sensibly affected with lesser evils and troubles, and yet to be hard and insensible for sin which is the greatest of evils. It would be our wisdom, therefore, when any other evils are upon us, to turn all our sighs,

Sin: The Greatest Evil

tears, and sorrows upon sin.

It is an aphorism in medicine, if a man bleeds vehemently in one place, they let him bleed in another and so turn the stream of blood another way. It should be our wisdom, when our souls bleed and our hearts mourn for other evils, to turn all those mourning affections upon sin. Let them run in the right channel.

Those tears must be wept over again which are not shed for sin. Sorrow is like Mercury's influence: good, if it is joined with a good planet, bad, if joined with a bad planet. It is not so much the sorrow as it is the ground and spring of sorrow. The object of it is to be taken notice of. Sorrow was naught in Judas, good in Peter; it was naught in Saul, good in David. In the one, worldly; in the other, godly — *"Worldly sorrow causeth death."* And such is all sorrow that does not have sin as its ground, grace for the principle, God for the end.

Where sin is apprehended to be the greatest evil, it will have the greatest sorrow, sorrow to exceed all other sorrows.

1. Though not ever in quantity and bulk, yet in quality and worth: a little gold is worth a great deal of earth and rubbish.

2. Though not in strength, yet in length and continuance: other sorrows are but like a land-flood, occasioned by a storm which, when it is over, the flood is down. This godly sorrow arises from a spring, and, having a fountain to continue it, is permanent when the

Sin: The Greatest Evil

other is gone. This is the difference between godly sorrow and the other.

The sorrows of God's people, which are spiritual, arise from a spring. Their worldly sorrows arise from a storm, a tempest. The sorrows of the wicked arise from their spiritual sorrows, arise from a storm, some present wringing of conscience, fear of wrath, and their worldly sorrows arise from a spring.

Where sin is apprehended to be the greatest evil, there it shall have the greatest sorrow, (1) a sorrow proportionable to the measures and greatness of sin, and (2) a sorrow proportionable to the merit and desert of sin.

As the merit of sin is infinite, so the sorrow for it must be an infinite sorrow. Infinite, I say, not in the act and expression, but in the desire and affection of the soul. He whose heart and eyes dry up together, whose expression in tears and affection of sorrow end together, though he has wept a sea of tears, he has not yet truly wept for sin. Where sorrow is godly, it has affections of mourning when the expressions of mourning cease because every drop of tears arises from a spring of tears within.

As every act of faith arises from a believing disposition, a habit of faith within, every act of love from a principle of love within, so every expression of sorrow arises from an affection of sorrow in the spirit. Hence we read, I Sam.7:6, that their sorrow is expressed by

Sin: The Greatest Evil

this metaphor, *"They drew water* (as out of a well) *and poured it out before the Lord."* Their eyes did not empty as fast as their hearts filled. Their eyes could not pour it forth as fast as their hearts yielded it up. All their expressions of mourning fell short of those affections of sorrow which were in the heart.

This is sorrow for sin: a sorrow proportioned to the measure, to the demerit of sin; a sorrow that exceeds all other sorrows, though not in quantity, yet in quality; though not in strength, yet in length and continuance.

Is sin the greatest evil? Then it calls out for the greatest hatred. Nothing is properly the object of hatred but evil, and not all kinds of evil, but sinful evil. Penal evils are rather the objects of fear than hatred, because these are improperly evil. Nothing indeed is evil but what makes us evil, and these may be a means to make us good and, therefore, are not properly evil and so an object of hatred.

Sinful evil is properly the object of hatred because this is properly evil and, being the greatest of evils, should therefore have the greatest of our hatred, Ps.92:10, *"You that love the Lord,"* see that you hate evil. It is not enough for you to be angry with sin and displeased with sin, for so a man may be with his friend, one whom he loves, for some discourtesy. Nor is it enough that you should strike sin, for so many do

Sin: The Greatest Evil

today and embrace it tomorrow. But you must endeavor to kill sin. Hatred labors after the "un-being" of that which it hates. Nothing but the destruction and blood of it will satisfy the soul that truly hates sin.

There is a great deal of error in men concerning this point. I might show you the secret deceits of the spirit concerning it in brief and how far those come short of a hatred of sin.

1. A man may fall out with a sinner by whom he has been drawn into sin and yet not hate the sin; execute the traitor and like the treason.

2. A man may fall out with himself for sin and yet not hate sin; when he has been inconvenienced by his sin which otherwise he liked well enough.

3. A man may fall out with sin and yet not hate sin; cast away the coal when he is burned with the fire that is in it, and yet not be offended with the blackness of it or the defilement which he gets by it.

If sin is the greatest evil, then it calls for the greatest care to avoid it. Men are naturally afraid to fall into evil. What study, what care, what endeavors to prevent evil? If you apprehended sin to be the greatest evil, there would be no less care to avoid sin. You would endeavor to walk closely and exactly with God, to beware of all the occasions, allurements, etc., which might draw you to sin. None are so secure but they may fall into sin if they neglect their Christian watch.

Sin: The Greatest Evil

Thus, where sin is apprehended to be the greatest evil, there will be the greatest care and circumspection against sin. Such a man is acquainted with the falls of others, which to him are not landmarks to walk by but sea-marks and rocks to shun. He is acquainted with the weakness and wickedness of his own heart and spirit and therefore watches. He knows he cannot trust any member alone without a guard upon it.

The eyes are full of sin: adultery, pride, envy, lusts of the eye, I John 2:16, and he cannot trust his eyes without Job's covenant, *"I have made a covenant with my eyes; why then should I think on a maid?"* Job 31:1.

The tongue is full of sin: of cursings, murmurings, revilings, vain communications, and there is no trusting it without David's bridle, Ps.39:7, *"I will keep my mouth, as with a bridle, that I offend not with my tongue."* He knows his own weakness and wickedness, and therefore dares not trust any member without his keeper.

Such a man is acquainted with the power and policy of Satan, who is, as Luther called him, a subtle enemy, whose temptations are called the depths of Satan, Rev.2:24; his devices, II Cor.2:11; his methods, Eph.4:14. He suits his temptations accordingly, too.

Such a one is acquainted with the danger and deceitfulness of sin, and how it is (1) deceitful in its object; (2) deceitful in its arguments; (3) deceitful in its pretences and excuses; (4) deceitful in its encroaches;

Sin: The Greatest Evil

and (5) deceitful in its promises. And therefore he will keep a holy circumspection, a humble, awful, jealous fear over his own spirit lest he should fall into sin. He looks on sin as his greatest evil, and his greatest care and endeavors are to avoid sin.

If sin is the greatest evil, then it should be our chief endeavor to get rid of sin. Every man would labor to be rid of an evil, and, the greater the evil, the greater is our desire to be rid thereof. Now sin is the greatest of evils. How much more then, should we labor and endeavor to be rid of the greatest of evils?

Alas! Alas! What are all other evils to the evil of sin, which makes our good evil? And yet to see the vileness of men's spirits, they would fain be rid of all other evils, but not sin. So Pharaoh said, "Take away this death, this plague." They complain of the evil caused, but not of the evil causing; of the evil punishing, but not of the evil punished. They howl under the present scourges and afflictions, but never lament the sin. They would fain be rid of the pain, but yet they would fain keep the tooth. Whereas, alas, until sin is removed, it is not in mercy but in judgment, and your present deliverance only reserves for you a more severe stroke. Where on the contrary, if sin is removed, the affliction will be removed. They are like the body and the shadow: remove the body and the shadow must be removed. Sin is the body and afflictions are its shadow.

Sin: The Greatest Evil

Or if the afflictions continue, if God takes away sin, the evil of the evil is taken away. Sin is the sting of every affliction. Sin is that which embitters every cross, and, sin being taken away, that which is vindictive is taken away and that which is medicinal and for salvation remains. It is more fruitful than penal. All for merciful ends and out of merciful respects when sin is taken away.

If sin is the greatest evil, then let us rather choose to fall into the greatest evil in the world than into the least evil of sin. All other evils have some good in them and are the objects of choice, in case we cannot avoid them, but we must admit of sin. Thus you see Moses did, as you may read in Heb.11. He chose rather to be afflicted with the people of God than to enjoy the pleasures of sin for a season. But now sin is all evil and no good, and there is nothing in the world that should make us choose sin.

Is sin the greatest evil? Let this, then, put us on to pity and pray for such who are under a state of sin. You pity sick friends, poor friends, undone friends. But alas! What are all these evils to the evil of sin? What is poverty? What is sickness? What is anything to the evil of sin? All these are but outward, this is an inward evil. All these are but of a temporal nature, death but a conclusion to them all, but this is of an eternal nature. All others will never make you the object of God's wrath and hatred. And therefore, spend some tears,

Sin: The Greatest Evil

put up some prayers for such as are under the state of sin. *"O,"* said Abraham, *"that Ishmael might live in Thy sight!"* So you say there is such and such a friend, a brother, a father, etc., who lies under sin, is in a state of sin. Oh! that You would pity their souls! Oh! that You would snatch them out of their state of sin!

If sin is so great an evil, then let us fall down and admire the greatness of God's patience in bearing with sinners and the greatness of God's mercy in pardoning sin. Here admire the greatness of God's patience in bearing with sinners. It may be you have been an unclean sinner, a drunken sinner, a swearing wretch, these twenty, thirty, forty, it may be threescore years or more. And has God spared you? Oh! Here see the wonder of God's patience.

If it were not that God is Almighty in the power of His patience, it would have been impossible that He would have spared you so long. He tells us so in Hos.11:9, *"I am God and not man—I will not enter into the city to destroy it."* So Mal.3:6, *"I am JEHO-VAH, I change not—Therefore ye sons of Jacob are not consumed,"* implying that if He had not been God, if He had not been Almighty in the power of His patience, they would certainly have been cut off long before this.

If men are provoked daily and irritated with injuries and do not come out to get revenge, we attribute it either to their pussillanimity or to their impotency;

Sin: The Greatest Evil

either to their lack of courage or lack of power. But it is not so with God. His patience is His power, Num. 14:17-18. When God had threatened to destroy them, Moses prayed to God to forbear them, and he calls that act of His patience no less than His power, *"Now I beseech Thee, let the power of the Lord be great, according as Thou hast spoken — the Lord is long-suffering, etc."* You see, He makes His patience to be His power. And so it is indeed, if you consider what sin is. I shall say no more of it than this which God said, Lev.26:21, it is contrary to God.

1. It is contrary to the works of God. As soon as God set up and perfected the frame of the world, sin gave a shrewd shake to all; it unpinned this frame and would liked to have pulled all in pieces again. Had it not been for the promise of Christ, all this frame would have fallen in pieces again.

If a man should come into a curious artificer's shop and should, with one blow, dash in pieces a piece of art which cost him many year's study and pains in contriving it, how could he bear with it? Thus sin did, and yet that God should forbear? Oh! Omnipotent patience!

2. But yet further, it is contrary to God's nature. God is holy, sin unholy; God is pure. sin is filthy, and therefore is compared still to the most filthy things in the world: to the poison of asps, to ulcers, sores, etc. If all the noisesome pollutions in the world met in one

Sin: The Greatest Evil

common sink, it would never equal the pollution of sin.

God is good, perfect good; sin is evil, universally evil. There is good in all other things, plague, sickness. Hell itself has a kind of good in it. None in sin. Sin is the practical blasphemy of all the name of God. It is the dare of His justice, the rape of His mercy, the jeer of His patience, the slight of His power, the contempt of His love. It is every way contrary to God.

3. It is contrary to the will of God. God bids us do this. Sin says, "I will not do it." "Sanctify My Sabbath," God says. "I will not sanctify it," says sin. Here is contradiction, and who can endure contradiction?

It is set down as a great piece of Christ's sufferings, Heb.12:3, that He endured the contradiction of sinners against Himself. Certainly it was a great suffering. How can a wise man endure to be contradicted by a fool? And here that Christ, who was the wisdom of the Father, should bear with such contradiction from fools, here was a great piece of suffering.

Now sin is a contradiction of God. It sets will against wisdom and the hell of a wicked will against a heaven of infinite wisdom. And that God should bear with such sinners? Here is a wonder!

You know in all the creatures, contrarity makes all the combustion. It makes all the war in nature, it causes one element to fight against another. Fire against water, water against fire. It will make the very stones to sweat and burst asunder.

Travel through the whole creation and you will not see any creature that can bear with its contrarity. And that God and sin should be in contrarity and yet the sinner live in the world? Here is a wonder, a wonder of patience.

Is sin so great an evil? Then let us fall down and admire the greatness of God's mercy in pardoning sin. You see how the prophet cries out and admires, Mic.7:18, *"Who is a God like unto Thee, that pardoneth iniquity, and passeth by the transgressions of the remnant of His heritage?"*

It is one of the greatest works that God does in the world to pardon sin, a work in which He declares all His glorious attributes: His wisdom, His power, His justice, His mercy, His holiness, and so on in pardoning sin.

Men who have cheap and slight thoughts of God's pardoning mercy have, thereby, an evident sign that they never had a pardon, never knew what it was, indeed, to have a pardon.

If ever any work in the world put God to it, then this of the pardon of sin. And if ever God intends you any good, He will instruct you and rectify your judgment in this touching the pardon of sin. Therefore God humbles men at their bringing in to raise up their esteem of a pardon, to advance the greatness of His own mercy in pardoning sin. And indeed, we should

Sin: The Greatest Evil

not need such great preparations and humiliations in coming to Christ if we had but greater thoughts of the pardon of sin. Men make no more of a pardon than to cry, "God, mercy!" Swear an oath and then say, "God, forgive me!" or say, "Lord, have mercy on me when I die!"

It was said of Lewis II, King of France, that he wore a crucifix in his hat and when he sinned he would but kiss his crucifix and then all was done. And so the Papists make it no more but a crucifix and a confession. Ah! My brethren, if ever God means good to you, He will make you know what a pardon is. In Is.55:7, when God would draw men up to show them a pardon, He calls them above all the world, *"My thoughts are not your thoughts, nor your ways My ways,"* says the Lord. "If they were, then I could not multiply pardons, but as the heavens are higher than earth, so are My thoughts above your thoughts, and My ways above your ways. I am infinite."

If God's creating mercy is so great, as David with doubled admiration sets out, Ps.8:1 and the last verses, *"O Lord, our Lord! How wonderful is Thy name in all the world, Who hast set Thy glory above the heavens."* What, then, is His pardoning mercy?

Lastly, is sin so great an evil? Then see what cause we have to humble our souls before God this day that we have had such slight thoughts of sin, who has thus judged sin to be the greatest of all evils. What slight

Sin: The Greatest Evil

thoughts have we of sin? We can swallow it without fear, we can live in it without sense, we can commit it without remorse. All of which shows that we have but slight thoughts of sin, we do not apprehend sin to be such an evil as indeed it is.

Now that you may be able to have some suitable concepts of sin to the greatness of it, that you may be able to see sin as exceedingly sinful, I will briefly present it to you in these six glasses.

1. Look upon it in the glass of nature which, though it is but a dim-glass, is a blown-glass. Sin has dimmed it, yet is this able to reveal a great deal of the evil of sin. The very heathens themselves have seen and judged many sins to be the greatest of evils.

Though spiritual sins were hidden from them, their light was not able to discover infidelity and gospel sins, yet moral sins they have discovered and have avoided them, and would hazard themselves, nay, and suffer, too, rather than commit such sins. The examples of Plato, Scipio, Cato, and many others will clear this. And all this was discovered by the glass of nature, done by nature, but not by mere nature fallen, but by nature well-husbanded, by nature improved, by the implantation of moral principles together with restraining grace and other common gifts of the Spirit.

The greatness of their hatred against sin, the greatness of their care to avoid sin, the greatness of their sufferings rather than committing sin might be enough to reveal to us the greatness of the evil of sin, but we will pass this by.

2. The second glass wherein you may see the greatness of sin is the glass of the Law, a glass which reveals sin in all its dimensions: the guilt, demerit, filthiness, and sinfulness of sin. Hence the Apostle, Rom.7:7, says, *"I had not known sin, but by the Law."* That is, I had not known sin to be as heinous as it is, I had not known sin in the wideness and latitude of it. I had not known the sinfulness of sin if it had not been for the Law, if the Law had not been a glass to reveal sin to me. This revealed sin in its greatness to David, Ps.119:96, *"I have seen an end of all Thy perfection, but Thy Law is exceeding broad,"* that is, by revealing the compass of sin in proportion to its wideness and greatness.

Oh! This will reveal to you more nakedness in one sin than all the world can cover; more indigency in one sin than all the treasures of created righteousness are able to supply; more obliquity and injustice in one sin, in a wandering thought, than all the deaths of men and annihilations of angels are able to expiate.

Search into the Law and you shall discover thousands of sins which fall under any one Law of God. Oh! Here is a glass!

3. Look upon sin in the glass of the griefs, woundings, piercings, and sorrows which the saints have found in their admissions and first entrance into the state of grace, in their relapsings and turnings again to

Sin: The Greatest Evil

folly.

For the first, see what groans and humiliations they have endured in their first admissions into an estate of grace: in Manasseh, II Chr.33:12; in Paul, Acts 9; in the converted Jews, Acts 2:37; when the nails pierced Christ, now stuck in their hearts as the arrow in the stag's side.

How many of the saints have there been who have been cast into a bed of miserable sorrow, lain bed-ridden under the stroke of justice perhaps for many years, and all of this for sin. No age is without a thousand examples of it.

Look upon the sorrows and breakings which the saints have endured upon their relapsing into sin. See in Peter, in David. Read what sad expressions he has in Psalm 6, from verse 1 to verse 7, and in Ps.32:3-5. So Psalm 51. How he complains that his soul is troubled, his bones are broken, his eyes are consumed with sorrows, his bed swims with tears! And all this for sin. Here is a glass wherein you may see the evil of sin to be the greatest evil. Yea, and the least sin, when God sets it on, will do all this.

Look upon sin in Adam and there see the greatness of it. That one sin of Adam has brought all the miseries, sickness, death, etc., upon all his posterity since that time. It has been the damnation of thousands of millions of men and still runs on. God's justice is still unsatisfied. If it were, there would be a stop. We

Sin: The Greatest Evil

should die no more, be sick no more, etc. Oh! Here you may see sin in its extensiveness.

Look upon sin in Christ. See there what humblings, what breakings, what woundings, what piercings, what wrath it has brought upon Christ Himself. It was that which mingled that bitter cup with such woeful ingredients, which, had we but sipped of it when it was so tempered, would have laid our souls under more wrath than all the damned in hell suffer. Christ bore pure justice for sin.

Nay, it made Him who was God as well as man, sanctified by the Spirit to that work, strengthened by the Deity, to sweat drops of blood, and even to struggle and seem to draw back and pray against the work of His own mercy, and to decline the business of His own coming into the world.

Ah! None knows but Christ, nor is a finite understanding able to conceive, what Christ underwent when He was to bear sin, and with that to wrestle with the infinite wrath and justice of the infinite God, the terrors of death, and the powers of the world to come. Here is a glass wherein you may see the greatness of sin, the wideness of sin, the guilt of sin, the demerit of sin, all of which are set out to the life in the death, sufferings, breakings, and woundings of the Son of God.

You that make light of sin, go to Christ and ask Him how heavy it was, that which you make so light

Sin: The Greatest Evil

which pressed Him to the ground. And the least sin would have pressed you and all the pillars of heaven to the bottom of hell forever.

A sixth glass: look upon sin in the damnation of the soul forever, that nothing would satisfy the justice of God but the destruction of the creature. No sickness, no prisons, no blood, no sufferings but the sufferings of hell! And those not for a time, but forever! Ah! See here the greatness of sin, which might be further amplified by the consideration of the preciousness of the soul, which sin ruins to all eternity. And therefore, would you know sin? Ask the damned what sin is? Lay your ear to hell and hear those screechings, those howlings, those roarings of the damned, and all this is for sin. Oh, they are dear-bought pleasures which must be thus paid for with everlasting pains.

Thus you see what sin is by all these glasses. And therefore, oh! how we ought to be humbled for our slight thoughts of sin, which is so great an evil!

USE

Now if it be so, then see what need we have to aggravate sin to the utmost in our confessions of sin, because all we can say of it will fall infinitely short of the heinousness of sin. You can aggravate no sin so high as to raise it above itself, as to make sin greater than it is. You can have no magnifying glass to greaten

Sin: The Greatest Evil

sin above the greatness of it. You have such glasses to make greater other things above their highness which are able to present small things as great, mean things of vast size, but you have no glass to multiply sin and make sin appear bigger than it is.

The sufferings of the saints, the sorrows of the saints, the sufferings of the damned are too short. The glass of the Law, the glass of Christ's sufferings (which is the greatest), these do not show sin greater than it is, they only reveal sin in its just proportions and dimensions.

It would not have been justice in God to have required more blood and to put His own Son to more suffering than sin deserved. How would this have stood with God's love, His pity and mercy to His Son, to have put Him to more than sin deserved? Though there is more than enough mercy for the greatest sinners, as the Apostle says in I Tim.1:14, yet there was not more than enough justice exercised upon Christ for the demerit and guilt of sin.

The death of Christ was an adequate ransom for our souls and sins, and yet there was a redundancy of merit, an overflowing of merit, in the satisfaction of Christ to ransom a thousand worlds more to that if need be. As sin is infinite in regard of the object, so satisfaction is infinite in respect of the merit. Hence Christ's death is not only said to be a satisfaction, but a purchase; not only a payment, but a purchase.

Sin: The Greatest Evil

It is a satisfaction to the justice of God for sin in full, and a purchase of all good things from the mercy of God to which His justice, in respect of the validity and worth of Christ's satisfaction, is bound to us, but this by way of digression.

See, then, what need there is to aggravate sin to the utmost, because we cannot multiply sin to the greatness of it. There will be many singular fruits of so doing: (1) this will breed shame and confusion of spirit for sin; and (2) this will make you advance and relish mercy better.

When the debt seems little, we are ready and apt to undervalue a pardon. But when sin seems exceedingly sinful, this makes us value mercy, prize a pardon. When sin is seen as the greatest evil, mercy and pardon will be apprehended as the greatest good.

This puts us into the nearest disposition to forsake sin. As he who extenuates sin is resolved to continue in sin, so he who truly aggravates sin desires to be rid of it. Besides, it is a dissatisfaction with ourselves when we consider how ill we have dealt with God. It produces self-judging and self-condemnation as we see in David, Ps.51. It will produce spiritual softness and tenderness of heart for sin, but this I must pass over.

Sin: The Greatest Evil

USE

If sin is the greatest evil, then it is the greatest mercy in the world to be rid of sin. The greater the evil is, the greater is the mercy to be rid of it. But now sin is the greatest evil. And therefore you shall see it set down as the only mercy that comes in by Christ, Matt.1:25, *"He shall be called JESUS, because He shall save His people from their sins."* As if all other things coming in by Christ were included in this one, *"He shall save His people from their sins."* He does not say He shall save His people from hell, but from sin; from no other evil in the world, and this is the greatest mercy.

When God would speak the utmost, even the greatest thought of mercy that ever came upon His heart, when He would set down the greatest work of mercy that ever the mercy of God wrought, He said no more than this, *"He shall save His people from their sins."* Sin was the utmost evil, and therefore the saving from sin was the greatest good. And hence David, Ps.32: 1-2, said, *"Blessed is he whose iniquity is forgiven, and whose sin is covered. Blessed is that man to whom the Lord imputeth not sin."*

Indeed, we have mean thoughts, cheap thoughts, of pardon of sin, and the reason is because we have slight thoughts of sin. But if God once opened our understandings and made us see the vastness and wide-

Sin: The Greatest Evil

ness of the evil of sin, and if He should join a feeling sense to that of sight and make us feel what sin is, if He should let but the least sparkle of His wrath fall upon our spirits for sin, it would make our faces gather blackness. We would quickly change our note and say, "Oh! Blessed and forever blessed are those whose iniquity is forgiven and whose sin is covered."

But lest I should seem to beat the air, we will therefore circumstantiate this mercy a little and you shall see the greatness of it. Though, indeed, it would be enough to tell you that sin is the greatest evil. Thence would necessarily follow that it is the greatest mercy in the world to be rid of sin, which will more full appear if we consider the following particulars.

First, then, the pardon of sin is the dearest-bought mercy, and that is something to show the greatness of the mercy. You know, the greater the sum is that is to be paid for the purchase of a thing (provided there is no lack of wisdom in the buyer nor lack of honesty in the seller), the greater still, and of more worth is the thing bought or purchased. But now this mercy, pardon of sin, was a mercy dear-bought. It cost blood, Matt.26:28, and that *"not the blood of bulls and goats, for that it was impossible it should take away sins,"* as the Apostle has it in Heb.10:4. What was it, then? Why, it was the precious blood of Christ, I Pet.1:18-19, *"You were not redeemed with corruptible things, as silver and gold, from your vain conversation; but with the*

Sin: The Greatest Evil

precious blood of Christ, as of a Lamb without blemish and spot." And this, the blood of God, Acts 20:28, *"Feed the church of God, which He hath purchased with His own blood."*

Now sit down and think what a mercy that must be which is the price of blood, and that of the Son of God. There was no lack of wisdom in the buyer, He could not be over-reached, He knew the worth of the commodity. Nor was there lack of justice or goodness in the Seller. He was just and would not take one drop of blood more than the thing was worth. And He was a Father, too, and therefore would not put His Son to more sufferings and require more than the thing was worth.

This is the purest mercy of all others, the pardon of sin, a mercy that comes from the heart and good will of God to you. God may give you all other things and hate you. You may be rich and yet reprobates; great in the world here and be damned hereafter. Dives may have wealth, Herod eloquence, Saul command, Agrippa glorious apparel; a man may do wickedly and yet prosper. These things are not truly good nor truly evil. If good, the wicked should not have them; if evil, the saints should not have them. These are such things as God reaches from His hand, not from His heart. They are general favors, not special love. But this is a peculiar favor, the saints' peculiar, pure mercy, a mercy that came from the bowels of mercy, the heart

Sin: The Greatest Evil

of mercy.

This is the freest mercy of all others, pardon of sin. There was nothing to engage God to do it, nor was there anything we could do to purchase it. All our prayers, our tears, our services, could not purchase the pardon of one sin if, for the active part we could do as much, and, for the passive part, we could suffer as much as all the saints put together have done from the beginning of the world to this day.

If we should weep as many tears as the sea holds drops, if we should humble ourselves as many days as the world has stood minutes from the creation, etc., all this would be too short to purchase the pardon of one sin, though we did all without sin.

But, alas! All that we can ever do is so far from striking off any former score that we do but set ourselves further in debt thereby! So far are we from purchasing a pardon that we do but increase our treason. We must not work that we may be justified, but we are justified that we may work. So that is the freest mercy. And therefore in Scripture you read it all attributed to grace, Tit.3:7, *"We are justified freely by His grace;"* Rom.3:24, *"Being justified freely by His grace;"* Rom.4:5, *"God justifies the ungodly."* There is no motive in us, all is from God. And you shall see it plainly, one place for two, in Is.43:23-25: *"Thou hast bought Me no sweet cane with money, nor hast thou made Me drink with the fat of thy sacrifices, but thou*

Sin: The Greatest Evil

hast made Me serve with thy sins, thou hast wearied Me with thy iniquities. I, I am He that putteth away thy iniquities, for My own name's sake, and will not remember thy sins."

Would a man have expected this? This shows freeness when not only do we have no deservings, but contrary deservings, *"Thou hast wearied Me with thy iniquities."* Oh, infinite, oh, freest mercy! God is merciful only because He will be merciful.

It is an entitling mercy, a mercy that entitles you to more good than I am able to express or you are able to conceive. It is a mercy that interests you in all other mercies. It entitles you to all the good on earth, to all the glory of heaven. Nay, it is a mercy-making mercy, a mercy that makes all other things mercy to you.

Good things are mercies. Your riches, your greatness, your possessions, your husbands, your wives, children, etc., all these things are not blessings until they are joined with a pardon, and that makes them all blessings. Nay, not only good things, but evil things are mercies to you. Pardon of sin makes poverty, affliction, sickness, and even death itself a mercy. Like the unicorn's horn, it takes away the venom and poison of every water. Like the philosopher's stone, it turns all into gold. So said the Apostle, *"All things work together for good unto them that love God."* A sanctified cross is better than an unsanctified comfort. A loss in mercy is better than an enjoyment in wrath.

Sin: The Greatest Evil

You are never able to make it good, that God bestows anything in mercy, until sin is forgiven. Guilt of sin upon you turns the nature of things, and makes those things which are good in themselves evil to you.

It is an irrevocable mercy. God may give other mercies and call for them again. Indeed, other things are rather lent than given: lent husband, lent wife, etc. Hence they are said to be but talents in our hands and we are stewards of them for a time. God may call for them when He pleases or we may forfeit them and lose them.

How often do we forfeit and lose good things because of our unworthy walking in the enjoyment thereof? Hos.2:8-9, *"I will take away My corn in the time thereof, My wine and My flax in their season."* It was God's, and would you know the reason? See in the former verse. Because they did not acknowledge God as the Giver of them, but bestowed them on Baal as though he had given them.

But now this mercy is an irrevocable mercy, a mercy that God never recalls, a mercy God never repents of. The gifts and graces of God are without repentance, and it is a mercy never forfeited.

We may forfeit the sense of a pardon, we may forfeit the comfort of a pardon, nay, we may forfeit the knowledge of a pardon as it was with David, but we shall never forfeit a pardon. If all this foreseen could not hinder God from giving out a pardon, neither can

Sin: The Greatest Evil

it make God repent of a pardon when He has given it.

Now the stability of the mercy is that which adds a great deal of worth to the mercy. As things that are evil, so much more things that are good, are heightened from the consideration of the continuance of them, the stability and lastingness of them. Now this is a stable mercy. Take but one place, Is.54:8-10, *"For this is as the waters of Noah unto Me: for, as I have sworn that the waters of Noah should no more go over the earth: so have I sworn that I will not be wroth with thee, nor rebuke thee,"* yet further, *"for the mountains shall depart, and the hills shall be removed: but My kindness shall never depart from thee, nor shall the covenant of My peace be removed."*

This is the difference between the Covenant of Works and the Covenant of Grace. The one is temporary, the other is eternal. It is a temporary covenant though an eternal rule. The other is eternal and immutable.

Pardon of sin is a universal mercy, the womb of mercy, a productive mercy. All other mercies grow upon this tree of forgiveness of sin. It is a tree, the root whereof is in Christ, and the fruit thereof are all good things on earth and in heaven. There are seven glorious fruits of pardon of sin which I will but name, and so come to the last use.

1. Reconciliation with God, II Cor.5:19, admission into His favor. He who before was an enemy has now

Sin: The Greatest Evil

become your Friend, for nothing makes God an enemy but sin. And such a Friend He is who will be a Friend in life, a Friend in death when all other friends forsake, and a Friend after death.

2. Adoption of children, which follows upon our pardon in justification.

3. Access to God as to a Father with childlike boldness. Sin was that great gulf between God and us. Sin was the partition-wall between God and us. Now sin being pardoned, this partition-wall is taken down and there is access to God, and access with boldness.

4. Acceptation of our services. Until sin is pardoned, there is no acceptation of any service. Until our persons are accepted and reconciled, our performances are abominable. But now sin being pardoned, here is acceptance for all our services. He drinks the milk as well as the wine, Canticles 5:1, and eats the honeycomb with the honey, etc.

5. Sanctification of every condition to us when sin is removed, which was the curse of all.

6. Support under crosses upon removal of sin, which was in all the heaviest burdens.

7. Participation of all the privileges of the Covenant. These are the inseparable fruits of pardon.

There are others, such as peace, joy, comfort, Rom. 5:1, which indeed are not so much fruits of pardon as fruits of assurance of pardon; not the text, but the more remote fruits of pardon.

Sin: The Greatest Evil

USE

Lastly, is sin the greatest evil in the world? Oh, then! Let us above all other things in the world labor to get ourselves rid of sin. Get a pardon of sin. Say with David, *"Oh! Take away the iniquity of Thy servant."* What will the enjoyment of all other good profit you if your sins are not pardoned? What profit had Dives of his wealth? Saul of his kingdom?

It is a thing greatly to be lamented to see how active and serious men are about removing other evils and the purchasing and procuring of other goods, but yet how slight, how superficial they are about getting pardon of sin.

Your person is under the guilt of sin. You stand as a condemned man and woman. And God has given you time, and that time is not a time of reprieval only, but it is a time that God has afforded you to get a pardon. And it cost no less than the blood of Christ to procure you this time. It was that which made a stop of the present proceedings of God's justice against you, else you would have been in hell long ago. And will you squander away this time? Will you neglect this business? Will you eat away, sleep away, nay, drink away, sin away such a pardon?

If there was a man condemned to die, who was reprieved out of mercy that he might procure his pardon, and if the King was willing to grant him

Sin: The Greatest Evil

a pardon, would you not think the man deserved to die who now spent his time in drinking, reveling, and the like? Why, this is your case.

But yet, there is another sort that will seek for a pardon, but they seek it coldly. They seek it formally, they seek it slightly and superficially. They seek it as if they had no need of it, as if they could do well enough, though they lacked a pardon.

There is a great deal of dallying with God about this great business. Most men in the world do but trifle with God about it. I will name you five or six sorts of men who are triflers with God in this main and concerning matter, and these are not the lowest, either. I shall not deal now with your debauched people, but such as seem to do something for a pardon.

1. Such who will seek and perhaps cry earnestly, but yet still continue in the practice of those sins for which they beg a pardon. I do not speak now of sin of course: sins of daily incursion, sins of infirmity, weakness and imperfections in duty. These the best, notwithstanding their daily praying for pardon, do yet too often fall into. But I speak of grosser sins, sins wounding and gashing the conscience. And this is a fearful thing, dallying with God.

What would you think of such a man who should come to beg a pardon and yet, before the pardon is given out, should run to commit new acts of treason? This is your case. I see many of you living in a course

Sin: The Greatest Evil

of sin: drinking ale, heavy drinking, swearing. I am ashamed to name them.

Do you pray for a pardon? Or do you not pray? If you do not pray, you are no better than atheists. And do you pray for a pardon and yet live in the practice of those sins you beg pardon for? Oh! What fearful dallying with God is here!

Oh! You little think what a strong tie this is against sin, to pray for the pardon of sin. What? Have you been confessing sin, humbling your souls for sin, begging for pardon of sin, and no sooner turn your backs upon God, but return to sin? Ah! This is fearful dallying, indeed!

And this is a fearful aggravation of sin. You think to have something come in for your days of humiliation, for your prayers of pardon. You think there is some good in it. Why? You have begged a pardon, though you have sinned; yet you have prayed, and therefore hope that, notwithstanding your sins, God will hear your prayers. But do you live in sin and confess sin? Do you practice sin and yet pray for pardon of sin? Do you commit sin and yet humble yourself for sin? Oh, these are great aggravations of sin. These add more weight to sin!

Do you think it would be an extenuation or an aggravation for a malefactor to beg a pardon, and yet run to the same rebellion again? Would he think to lessen his sin because he had formerly begged a

Sin: The Greatest Evil

pardon? No, certainly! He would look upon this as a greater aggravation. Why, this is your case!

And this, you shall see, was Israel's spirit which was so displeasing to God, Jer.3:4, *"Thou art my Father, and the Guide of my youth."* They gave God good words, compassed Him about with good expressions, but, said the Lord, *"This hast thou done, and yet done as much evil as thou couldst,"* verse 5.

2. A second sort who dally with God are those who seek the pardon of some sins, but yet keep up the love and liking of others. You are, it may be, pinched and troubled for some gross sins, and you beg a pardon for them when, it may be, there is some running issue of corruption within which you overlook, some secret haunt of villany that your heart runs out after which you cannot leave, which you have no mind to part with.

Oh, you vain man! You may cry all your life and shall never get good. You may pray as long as you will That one sin, kept with love and liking, will turn all your prayers into sin. God will never regard the prayers of a sin-regarding sinner, Ps.66:18, *"If I regard iniquity in my heart, the Lord will not hear me,"* though I should never act it in my life.

If you but knew the tenor of the Covenant of Grace and Mercy, the strictness of the gospel, and the severity of mercy itself against sin, you would see the impossibility of having one sin forgiven as long as one

Sin: The Greatest Evil

sin is unforsaken! Justification and sanctification, God's forgiving and our forgoing, are equally as large, one as the other. As God justifies from the guilt of sin, so He sanctifies from the corruption of all sin. Grace in God forgives all sin, and grace in us makes us forgo all sin. Where sin is forgiven, there sin is forsaken.

3. A third sort are they who seek a pardon of sin without sense of sin, who seek forgiveness of sin without remorse for sin; men who are never troubled with any sense, with any compunction of heart for sin.

Would you not take it for dallying with you if one greatly offended you and came to desire your forgiveness without any sense of it or remorse for it? What do you think God will do?

This is certain, without blood there is no remission of sin, as the Apostle speaks. Christ was wounded, and you must be wounded, too, before you have a pardon. Christ bled, and conscience must bleed before ever He will give a pardon. Will a man in good earnest beg a pardon who was never attached for treasons, or so much as is thoroughly sensible that he is guilty of it?

4. A fourth sort are such as cry for forgiveness, but yet never look after their prayers. Would you not think it a slighting if a man who had offended you should come and beg a pardon, and as soon as he had said a few words to you should turn his back and go away, and never expect nor wait for an answer from you?

Why do you deal thus with God? You put up

Sin: The Greatest Evil

prayers but do not look after them. He who begs in earnest, oh! he will diligently observe what answer, what return God makes. He will observe what word of comfort God lets fall, what intimations God will afford to his spirit, and will be exceedingly cautious of them, as you see Benhadad's servants did, I Kings 20:31-33. After they had put up their request, the text says, *"The men did diligently observe whether anything would come from Ahab, and did hastily catch at it."* So should we do. Come with sackcloth, put up our prayers with remorse, and when that is done, when we have received our prayers, let us wait upon our prayers, to see what intimations we shall receive from heaven. Thus David, Ps.85:8, *"I will hear what God the Lord will speak; for He will speak peace to His people, and to His saints."* Ps.5:3, *"In the morning will I direct my prayers, and will look up."*

5. A fifth sort who dally with God are they who follow not their prayers with endeavors to get assurance that their sins are pardoned; who search not into the Covenant of Grace, acquaint not themselves with the promises of grace, search not into the Word of grace, frequent not the means of grace. These men dally who frequent not the Word, Sacraments, etc., and such like means for the assurance of pardon.

FINIS

-68-

The Conversion of a Sinner

Explained and Applied

from Ezekiel 33:11,
" *...Turn ye, turn ye, from your*
evil ways, for why will ye die,
O house of Israel?"

by Nathaniel Vincent,
Minister of the Gospel

(First Published in 1669)

The Conversion of a Sinner

THE DEDICATION

To His sacred and most glorious Majesty, the God of Heaven and earth, the KING OF KINGS, and LORD OF LORDS; who is much more above the highest potentates and Emperors in the world than they are above their meanest slaves!

Almighty Lord! To You I dedicate my book, to whom I have devoted myself, all that is good therein, it is Your own, and if it does any good, to You I must ascribe the praise. The instrument indeed might be ashamed and discouraged if he did not know that You can work as well by weak means as by strong. Nay, sometimes You make choice of weak on purpose that the flesh may not glory, but the excellency of the power may be of You alone.

It was most free and rich grace (which eternity itself will be short enough to admire and adore) that I myself was pitied, who once lay as much polluted in my blood as any other; who had run so far in the broad way and had sinned myself so near the destruction which is everlasting! But if I am not only made a convert, but also made use of to convert others, my obligation will be heightened, which is infinitely vast already, to show forth Your praise.

'Tis the desire of my soul, O Lord, that Your kingdom be advanced and that the dominion which sin and Satan have usurped may be overthrown. Since Your

The Conversion of a Sinner

yoke is easy and Your government so sweet, so gracious, why should not Your subjects also be most numerous? Gird Your sword upon Your thigh, oh most mighty One! And ride forth conquering and to conquer; and Your right hand shall teach You terrible things. Let Your arrows be sharp and Your Word pierce like a two-edged sword, and let the whole world, either by conversion or subversion, but especially by conversion, fall under You!

You are the God of the spirits of all flesh, is there anything too hard for You? When the devil sinned against You (and thereby became a devil), You easily threw him out of heaven and shackled him in chains of darkness. And can you not as easily throw him out of those sinner's hearts which he has possessed and filled, and pull down all his strongholds? And as for sin, though it be so mighty a thing that Adam in innocency was overcome by it, that angels in heaven could not stand before it, yet You are able and have promised to subdue it. Oh, show Your power and grace!

Since Your mercy is so great, why should there be so few partakers of mercy? Since Your Son is able to save to the uttermost, why should so small a number be saved by Him? Since the New Jerusalem is so spacious, why should hell fill so exceedingly fast? Oh, let Your special love be more generally manifested! Let Your healing and Your saving grace run in a much

The Conversion of a Sinner

broader channel and let your tents be enlarged and let them stretch forth the curtains of Your habitation! Let not so many souls be the devil's prey, which are of greater value than the world, and which are capable of loving, admiring, and glorifying You forever! Answer, O my God, such desires as these, so far as they are consistent with the secrets of Your counsel and Your ways and judgments, which are unsearchable and past finding out!

Let Your gospel continue in this land of England! Let the sun of righteousness shine forth in greater strength and glory, dispel the mists of error, and chase away the night of ignorance! Let not the sea be more full of water than this land is of the knowledge of Your glory! As long as there is a church on earth, let there be a church in England! And let the lamp of Your Word shine clearly among us as long as the sun and the moon shall shine in the firmament!

You who have the hearts of all in Your own hand, incline some to read these following sermons, and let all that read them be the better by them. Let them understand in this their day the things which concern their peace and obey Your call to turn before You come to this resolution to call and cry no more after them! Oh, let none grow more blind by the light's shining in their eyes! Let none grow harder by the means which were designed to soften them! Let not the Word of Life prove unto any a deadly savour! Let

The Conversion of a Sinner

some souls date their conversion from their reading this book, and let those who are converted be further strengthened by it. Encourage Your servant more and more by making his labors more abundantly successful, who has resigned and given up himself to You, and whose greatest honor and truest happiness is to be,

Yours Forever,

NATHANIEL VINCENT

The Conversion of a Sinner

THE EPISTLE TO THE READER

Reader! As soon as you have looked on, immediately look off again and look up to heaven! How can you see to read with any profit unless the Father of lights opens your eyes and gives you an understanding heart? He can show you wonders in the most common truths which before you were unacquainted with. Those doctrines that are most usually preached, as your judgment may yet more fully be informed about them, so I am sure your affections need to be stirred up to bear some more proportionable suitableness unto the weight and concernment of them.

It has moved my sorrow, and almost my indignation, to see how many truths are nauseated by some professors. And yet, alas, these very truths, though they have heard them often, they do not know them as they ought to know. As to any heart-affecting and operative knowledge, these persons who fancy and conceit themselves so very intelligent are very grossly ignorant. Their consciences are stupid and they were never brought under the power of the Word which is preached to them. Duties, though plainly and frequently pressed, are neglected, and sins which they commonly hear reproved are yet, notwithstanding, more commonly given way to.

You who cannot like a discourse unless your fancy is pleased and your itching ear clawed, what just reason you have to question whether your nature has been renewed. For they who have been born again desire the sincere milk of the Word (though there is a little mixture of what is human) that they may grow thereby.

Reader! Are you grossly ignorant and ungodly? How much, then, does it concern you to use those means which are appointed for the attaining of knowledge? Without knowledge your heart cannot be good, nor you yourself in a safe estate. You are gone astray. Oh, turn immediately lest the next step you take be into the grave and hell! It is but small security not to perceive your danger. It is but a pitiful happiness to be ignorant of your misery, for this very ignorance increases your danger and will make your misery the more unavoidable. Sin is such a thing as none ever repented of their parting with. Therefore, be persuaded to deny your former ungodliness and worldly lusts and to live soberly, righteously, and godly in this present evil world.

If you are a professor but not a practicer of religion, consider, 'tis not a feigned conversion, but a turning with the whole heart upon which life is promised and assured. If you have a form of godliness without the power, what does this prove but that you have more of the atheist in you? Surely you think that the Lord does not regard and will not punish, at least to you He will be partial. I wonder how you dare come

The Conversion of a Sinner

so often into His presence, so near His ark where His jealousy is hottest, and so frequently engage in duties of His worship, some sin or vanity all the while keeping your heart away from Him.

But if you are indeed converted, oh, get nearer unto God and turn more and more to Him. Grace is so excellent a thing that I think you should be restlessly importunate for a greater measure of it. The more you follow on to know the Lord, the better you will love Him, and the more unwilling you will be to leave Him and return again to folly.

Conversion is a nail which the prophets of old were hammering upon perpetually. Our Lord and His apostles endeavored to drive this nail home, and God of late has not only sent His ministers to ply this business but has taken the hammer of judgments to make this nail to enter. Now the stronger the resistance is that we make, we must expect more strokes from this hammer. We have seen lately days of great calamity and affliction, and yet they have, in some sense, also been days of grace. Therefore, temporal judgments have been sent that spiritual mercies might be prized and eternal judgments might be prevented.

God has had a design of love at the bottom of all His severities. Let us comply with it, for if we still walk contrary, He has threatened in fury to chastise us seven-fold more than as yet He has chastised us. And I may well tremble to think of those judgments which

The Conversion of a Sinner

will be seven times worse than the plague and fire. But if we learn wisdom and instruction by His correction, and turn unto Him that has smitten us, we shall find the expressions of His favor and lovingkindness far greater than ever were the signs of His displeasure.

N.V.

Ezekiel 33:11, latter part

"...turn ye, turn ye from your evil ways;
for why will ye die, O house of Israel?"

It is not very easy to discern whether man revealed greater folly in departing from God at first or whether his folly is now more inexcusable in refusing to return to Him. At first he knew by blessed experience how good it was to be near his Maker, to enjoy the light of His countenance in the state of innocency, and yet he ventured to go away. Now he feels the effects of his apostasy, for sin has loaded him with various miseries, calamities, vexations, and yet how hardly is he persuaded to come back again? The children of men are easily induced to yield to Satan as if it were their interest to give themselves into the hands of a murderer. But the Lord, besides whom there is no Saviour, may call, and call with frequency, with earnestness, yet call in vain. Their hearts are dull, their ears are deaf, they will not hearken to Him.

It can never be sufficiently lamented that sin has made many madmen in the world. Life and death, blessing and curse are set before them, yet death is chosen before life, the most astonishing and intolerable curses are embraced, when blessings of the

The Conversion of a Sinner

highest and most durable nature are rejected.

Hence it is that the Lord expostulates, not only in reference to sin, but in reference to punishment. He not only asks why you will venture to transgress, but also why are you so forward to die, O house of Israel?

The prophet, in the beginning of this chapter, is appointed by the Lord as a watchman over the house of Israel. He is commanded to lift up his voice when he sees the revenging sword drawn forth and coming to cut the ungodly off for their ungodliness and unless he calls to the wicked to turn and live, he is an accessory to their death. Their blood will be required at his hand. Being thus commissioned, he is commanded to stop the mouths of evildoers who cavil and reply against their Maker and charge God foolishly.

It seems there was a controversy about at whose door the destruction of sinners was to be laid. The house of Israel very peremptorily and boldly laid the blame on God, saying that the way of the Lord is not equal. But the God of mercy and truth vindicates Himself from that undeserved imputation, professing that if sinners were not perversely bent on their own ruin, destruction would be escaped. By His life, He swears that the death of the wicked pleases Him not. Therefore in the text, His voice is loud and doubled, *"Turn ye, turn ye from your evil ways,"* and the saddle is set upon the right horse. Men's own wills are the cause of their own woe, *"Why will ye die, O house of Israel?"*

The Conversion of a Sinner

The words express a very pathetic and serious call, wherein observe:

1. The persons called: the house of Israel;
2. To what they are called: they are called to turn;
3. The urgency of this call, which appears in the doubling of it: *"Turn ye, turn ye."*
4. From what they must turn: from their evil ways;
5. The argument used to prevail, which has an abundance of holy rhetoric in it: *"Why will ye die?"*

Without turning, death is certain. Satan may say to the posterity as he did once to our first parents, *"Ye shall not surely die,"* but this will be found true, *"Those shall be turned into hell,"* (Ps.9:17) who will not turn to God. Thither 'tis that evil ways all have a tendency. There are several paths in the broad way, but in death, the second death, they all conclude and meet. Therefore, the Lord is brought in, pitying sinners and pleading with them.

Why will you die? Is it because I am so speedy in revenging? You know I am slow to anger, and by experience you have found Me so, else My wrath had long before this broken forth upon you. Or is it because I am inexorable, not to be entreated when once

The Conversion of a Sinner

provoked? Why, I have proclaimed Myself ready to forgive and plenteous in mercy unto all that call upon Me. Or is it because you have never heard of the way and means of recovering life and flying from the punishment you have deserved? How often have I sent My prophets that you might be brought to believe, to repent, and to obey? But still your neck is an iron sinew. You are resolved to rush on in sin. If you perish, you may thank yourselves. If you are destroyed, it is because you choose destruction.

Three doctrines the text affords us:

1. Evil ways are the ways of death.
2. The great reason why men die, and die forever, is because they will.
3. The Lord calls and calls again upon sinners to turn from their evil ways and live.

DOCTRINE 1. I begin with the first doctrine, that evil ways are the ways of death. As they are morally evil, so evil and destructive to them that walk in them. Indeed, these ways may seem right, but because of this they are not the less, but the more pernicious, Prov.14:12, *"There is a way that seemeth right to a man, but the end thereof are the ways of death."*

1. These evil ways many times accelerate and hasten temporal death. That was the sentence pronounced

The Conversion of a Sinner

upon man's fall, *"Dust thou art, and unto dust thou shalt return."* And how often by sin is the execution of that sentence speeded? We read of some not suffered to live out half their days, Ps.55:23. The reason is because they lived so wickedly. Those whose carcasses fell into the wilderness might have lived to possess the land of promise, but they sometimes murmured. Sometimes they committed idolatry, sometimes fornication, and at last the oath is sworn that they should not enter into Canaan. The intemperate and unclean, how do they waste their strength? How many diseases do they punish themselves with? And though so miserably unprepared for judgments, how do they hasten their departure out of this world to the tribunal of Him who judges righteously?

2. God is not to be found in those evil ways. In a spiritual sense, we are dead though alive while we walk here. The Ephesians are said to be dead in trespasses and sins while they walked according to the course of this world and had their conversation in the lusts of their flesh, Eph.2:2-3. If the life of the soul consists in being united to God, in being animated and acted upon by His Spirit, then iniquity that separates us from God, Is.59:2, must be granted a deadly thing.

3. These evil ways are the beaten path to hell's damnation, to that death which is everlasting. No one ever came to hell but through these ways, and there is not one who continues to walk in them without conversion but shall come there. The enemy upon the pale horse without a second is dreadful, but when hell follows immediately after him, alas! What hand can be strong? What heart can be able to endure? This second death is called by one of the Fathers "the death that is immortal," because the sinner is never put out of his pain; always tortured, but never quite dispatched. The fire still burns, but never totally consumes them whom it burns. The worm still gnaws, but is never satisfied.

Whither away besotted and blinded soul? Whither is it that you are making such post haste? Is it gain, delight, and happiness which you have in chase, that you seem to fly rather than run towards? Alas, no. It is in the broad way that you drive on so furiously. It is not gain, but loss; it is not pleasure, but pain; it is not happiness, but misery, aye, and the most extreme misery which you are pursuing. Oh, stop your course and go no further! Oh, leave this lower path, Prov. 15:24. The way to life is above to the wise that he may depart from hell beneath.

You see in what respects evil ways are the ways of death. Now the righteousness of God in punishing those with death who persist in these ways will be evident if the following things are considered:

A. These ways are expressly forbidden by Him that is the supreme Law-Giver, who has power to save and to destroy. For so mean a wretch as man is to

The Conversion of a Sinner

affront and despise that majesty and authority that is so infinitely above him justly deserves an infinite punishment. Besides, the Lord presents Himself to a sinner if he will forsake his evil ways and thoughts. Now if the sinner rejects that offer and prefers not only the empty world but the vilest lusts before the blessed God, let reason judge if it is not just that he should be eternally separated from Him. And this loss of God is properly the death spoken of, it is the very hell of hell.

B. Sinners are threatened with death. If therefore they will venture upon that which brings them under the lash of the threatenings, 'tis but just they should smart for that presumption. They are forewarned to flee from that wrath which is to come, but if they take no warning, that wrath will very justly overtake them. They cannot plead, either, that they knew not their Master's will, or that they were ignorant of the penalty following their rebelling against it. How often have those that enjoy the light of the gospel been informed that it is the will of God that they should sorrow and rend their hearts for sin? That it is the will of God that they should believe in His Son? That it is the will of God even their sanctification, I Thess.4? Nay, how often have they been foretold of the many stripes that must be endured by those that continue in willful disobedience? It is not unequal, then, since they made the Lord a liar by their unbelief, that He should vindicate His truth and cause them to feel those plagues and torments which thousands of times they were warned of but had no faith or fear concerning them.

C. As sinners are threatened because of their evil ways, so they are shown which is the way of life and peace and are very much preferred to walk in it. Assisting and strengthening grace is presented to them, but if neither that glory and immortality at the end of the way nor that help and grace which they have in the way are regarded, but the paths of destruction and misery (as they are called), Rom.3:16, are preferred, they indeed wrong their own souls. But God is righteous in destroying them.

The only use I shall make of this doctrine is to caution you against these evil ways that are the ways of death. You that have, through grace, left them, take heed of declining towards them. It has cost the saints dearly when they have stepped aside. Their falls have defiled them and broken their bones. And you that still resolve to walk in these ways, at last open your eyes and see where you are going. Upon reading these lines, make a stop without delay lest sudden death, sudden destruction, sudden damnation come upon you, and there is no possibility of escaping, I Thess. 5:3.

1. Let not the profit of these ways blind you. Riches are deceitful, they appear to be what they are not, and while we are eagerly pursuing these, we are gulled and cheated of far truer riches. We miss that

The Conversion of a Sinner

treasure in heaven that will never fail, Luke 12:33. Be not deluded by the unrighteous mammon. Satisfaction, ease, contentment may be promised, but you will be paid in trouble and vexation. Riches are likened by our Lord to thorns, partly because they choke the good seed of the Word, and partly because they pierce those that dote upon them with many sorrows. Take the balances of the sanctuary and weigh the gain that you get by walking in your evil ways with the loss that you both do and will sustain, and then it will be apparent that Satan's heart and the heart's plea of profit is very unreasonable. You gain earth but you lose grace. You gain gold but you lose God. You gain a little of the world, which you can keep but a very little while, but you lose your souls and a whole eternity of glory.

2. Let not the pleasure of these evil ways ensnare you. The pleasures of sin usually delight only the more brutish part of man, and how much does one that has a reasonable soul act below himself in minding those pleasures that are common even to the beasts themselves? Solomon had an abundance of them. Whatever his eyes desired he kept not from them, neither withheld he from his heart any joy, but he found them so mean, so low, so unsuitable, that in the midst of them he cried out, *"All is vanity and vexation of spirit,"* Ecc.2:10-11. Pleasures are delightful dreams, but how short are they? How soon does affliction, death, if not hell awaken? They that are lovers of pleasure more

than lovers of God, how inconsiderate are they of what they choose or what they refuse? Pleasures are the baits which cover sin and make it swallowed down with eagerness. They are the fatal potion which stupifies you and makes you lie senseless and be in extreme danger. They are the finer, and yet most strong cords whereby Satan draws men down to the chambers of death. Nay, they are the fuel that heats the burning lake, Rev.18:7, *"By how much she hath glorified herself and lived deliciously, so much torment and sorrow give her."* Oh, how will the voluptuous one day smart for all their pleasures!

3. Let not the multitude of those who walk in these evil ways confirm and harden you. Lot walked alone in the way of righteousness, though Sodom was generally defiled by an ungodly conversation. He would not follow a multitude to do evil. He that said, *"Straight is the gate and narrow is the way which leadeth unto life, and few there be that find it,"* Matt.7, surely never intended that His disciples should go in the beaten path of the world. Sinner, do not deceive yourself with this. You do what others do and you shall shift as well as they. You and they will fare alike indeed, that is, be turned into hell for your wickedness.

It will be no comfort there to have companions in your misery, but rather among the damned there will be a torturing grief and indignation at the sight of one another to consider what incarnate devils they were to one another's souls, and helped forward one another's condemnation. Upon this score, it might be that the rich man of Luke 16 was so unwilling that his brethren should come to the place of torment, because if he were damned for those sins which he in his lifetime had been accessory to, their company with him in hell would have but added to his woe. We used to say here, "The more, the merrier," but there it will be, "The more, the sadder." When God has all of His enemies in one place together and none of His people mingled with them, then all His wrath will be stirred up and all the vials of His fury poured down upon them. I have finished with the first doctrine, that evil ways are the ways of death.

DOCTRINE 2. The second doctrine is this: the great reason why men die and die forever is because they will. They will be the servants of sin though death is all the wages they shall certainly have for their toilsome and laborious service. Sinners will not be purged, Jer. 13, *"Woe unto thee, O Jerusalem, wilt thou not be made clean? When shall it once be?"* They will not be gathered under the wing of Christ though there is the only place of refuge, both from the rage of Satan and from the wrath of God, Matt.23:37, *"O Jerusalem! Jerusalem! Thou that killest the prophets and stonest them that are sent unto thee, how often would I have gathered thy children together, as a hen gathereth her*

The Conversion of a Sinner

brood under her wings, and ye would not." Nay, the wills of many who have often slighted the admonitions and calls of Moses and the Prophets are so desperately bent to sin that though they should see the flames and torments it makes others suffer, yet they would not be persuaded to forsake it, Luke 15:30-31, *"Nay, father Abraham, but if one went to them from the dead they will repent, and he said unto him, If they hear not Moses and the Prophets, neither will they be per-suaded, though one rose from the dead."*

My work in the opening of this doctrine will be, first, to demonstrate the truth of it, that men die because they will; secondly, to evidence that men's inability to do what is good, so often spoken of in Scripture, does not at all contradict this doctrine.

The arguments to demonstrate that men's own wills are the great cause of their death and perdition are these:

1. One argument shall be drawn from the natural corruption and depravation of the will of man. And wherein does this corruption lie but in the will's de-clining from God, the Fountain of life and peace, and inclining to what is evil, though the sinner (woe unto him) calls that evil good and imagines that to be sweet which will prove as bitter and poisonous as the very gall of asps unto him. Pelagians may liken the will of man unto a pure virgin, which in the first apostasy escaped deflowering, but it is certain, both from

The Conversion of a Sinner

Scripture and experience, that in the will original sin most shows itself. He that does not understand his heart to be desperately wicked, Jer.17:9, it is a sign that his heart deceives him and he is utterly unacquainted with his own heart. What unbelief, what pride, what alienation from the life of God, what enmity against the command which is holy, just, and good, Rom.7, is there in the will of a natural man? The will, then, being so utterly corrupted and bearing such sway as indeed it does, must hinder conversion to God and holiness, which it dislikes so much. And consequently, it has a great hand in the perdition of the children of men.

2. Another argument shall be drawn from the justness of God's reproof and anger. Certainly He would not so sharply reprehend them, His anger would not smoke so against them because of their stubborness and willfulness in their evil ways if they had a sincere will and lacked only the power to do that which is good. When the Lord inflicted judgments upon His ancient people, He speaks of their obstinancy, their refusing to hearken and be reclaimed, and this He does to vindicate the equity of His more severe ways of dealing with them. We read, II Kings 17:13, 14, 18, that the Lord testified against Israel by His prophets and seers saying, *"Turn ye from your evil ways and keep My commandments. Notwithstanding, they would not hear, but hardened their necks like the neck of their fathers, which did not believe in the Lord their God."*

The Conversion of a Sinner

Now upon this willfulness followed, and that very justly, God's anger and their destruction. Therefore, the Lord was very angry with the children of Israel and removed them out of His sight.

In the second place, I am to prove that men's ability to do that which is good does not thwart this doctrine that their sin and misery is to be laid at their will's door. The Holy Ghost, that He might humble the children of men, beat down the opinon they have of their own power and righteousness and made them use the speech of the prophet in Is.45:25, *"Surely in the Lord have I righteousness and strength,"* incalculating this, that man, in his sinful and degenerate state, is unable to do that which is spiritually good. Therefore, we are said to be without strength, Rom.5:6. *"We are not sufficient of ourselves to think anything as of ourselves, but our sufficiency is of God,"* II Cor.3:5. We are said to be faint and to have no might, Is.40:29, and our Lord plainly tells us, John 15:5, *"Without Me ye can do nothing."* But for all this, though we lack a power to do good, our wills are blamed for the evil which is done by us.

It must not be imagined that the Scripture mentions the sinner's inability to do good to put an excuse in his mouth for doing evil, but to drive him to Christ who can strengthen him to do all things, Phil.4:13. It is true, man is unable, but withal he is unwilling to do what God requires of him, though tending to his own

The Conversion of a Sinner

welfare. The reason why he continues in sin and is undone by it is not only because he cannot convert himself, but also, and that principally, because he is unwilling to be converted. This will be made further to appear in these particulars:

1. Sinful man imagines himself able to turn from his evil ways. He defers his repentance as if he could turn to God at an hour's warning. Now that he does not do what he thinks he can, his own will must be the impediment, and this he must blame if so be that he perishes.

2. Sinful man will not do what he is really able to perform. One talent he has, but he will not trade with it. Many sins that expose him to wrath and vengeance he might abstain from if he would, but alas, he is voluntarily a slave to them, and is pleased with his servitude. The adulterer willfully goes to the harlot's house, the unrighteous worldling willfully gets dishonest gain. Therefore, it follows that these willfully destroy themselves.

A natural man can do that which is good as to the matter, though he fails in the manner of doing it. He can pray, hear, read, but he willfully omits these duties, and so willfully subjects himself to the curse that his threatened upon his omission. He will not do what he really can and, surely, if his power were enlarged, it would not be used. He that can well spare it and refuses to give a penny to the poor, we may conclude that, though he could spare it, he would be unwilling to give a pound. In like manner, a natural man who will not do what he can to be saved, which is but little, were his power greater, he would not do more in order to salvation.

3. Sinful man is sorry that he is able to do so much. He wishes that he were totally impotent that it might serve as an excuse for him. This shows the wickedness of his will. Further, he will not use the means by which grace and strength are conveyed. He will not wait and call upon God. He will not seek unto Him for the accomplishing of the promises made in the gracious covenant. Nay, he willfully resists the Spirit when He comes to work on him. He would rather be let alone in sin. That's the language of the ungodly ones, Job 21:14, *"They say unto God, depart from us, for we desire not the knowledge of Thy ways."* The wicked man, though he may cavil that he lacks power, yet this lack of will to be turned and live is that which mainly ruins him. And all those high thoughts and reasonings against God, as if He were a hard Master, as if His ways were not equal, how will a man be ashamed of them at the Great Day, when conscience shall fly in his face and in good sadness reproach him with this? He was often warned and called upon, but would not turn that he might have life.

The Conversion of a Sinner

THE APPLICATION FOLLOWS

USE 1. Of information in these particulars.

1. Do men die forever because they will? Then who are you, O man that charges God with destruction? Surely herein you charge God foolishly. As He delights not in your sin, so neither in your death. The malefactor must not be angry with the Judge for passing a sentence of condemnation upon him, but he ought to blame himself for doing that for which he deserves to be condemned. How often has the Lord called but you have refused? How often has He stretched forth His hand all the day long, but all the day long you have been disobedient and contrary? How speechless will this make you when He comes to judge the world in righteousness?

2. Do men die forever because they will? Then the death of the wicked is most just and righteous. It is but equal that the willing slaves of sin that would not become the Lord's freemen should be fettered in chains of darkness. The offender that refuses a pardon offered justly, nay, doubly deserves to have judgment executed, both because of his offense and because he slights mercy. The patient who thrusts away the physician who would heal him of a sore distemper very well deserves to die for it, and the sinner who will not turn to God, who rejects the Lord Jesus who is able both to pardon and to heal him, though he perishes

The Conversion of a Sinner

and is condemned, yet he is not in the least wronged.

3. Do men die forever because they will? What a torture will it be to them in hell to think it was their own willfulness which brought them thither? Such reflections such as these will be as so many poisoned daggers to pierce the very soul of a damned reprobate. What ailed me to prove a devil to myself? What ailed me to side with Satan for the bringing about of my own destruction? What frenzy was this to make the whips myself with which I am to be lashed, to kindle the flames with my own hands in which I must dwell and burn forever?

USE 2. Shall be of caution: take heed of willful sinning, which is the high road leading to death. Take heed also lest you content yourselves with a seeming willingness to escape destruction.

1. Let me caution you against willful sinning. The more of the will which is involved in transgression, the more provocation. Therefore, David is so earnest to be kept from presumptuous sins which he knew because presumptuous sins are so great, Ps.19:13. In a land and time of light, take heed of being willfully ignorant. In the midst of helps and encouragements to duty, take heed of sloth, which is a fault of the will, but be a follower of them who through faith and patience inherit the promises, Heb.6:12. Let no sin be loved, pleaded for, lived in. Let not the pleasing taste make you venture upon any forbidden fruit. Let not the fine-colored skin make you to hug any serpent in your bosom which will sting you to death.

2. Let me caution you against that which is only a seeming willingness to turn from sin and escape destruction.

A. An idle, industrious will is only a seeming will. A lazy wish to be saved, where there is no serious using of the means of salvation, signifies nothing but that you are grossly ignorant and stupid: ignorant of the worth of salvation and stupidly insensible of your own danger.

B. A will for the future is only a seeming will. Most of them who go on in their evil ways have a will to leave them hereafter, but this only shows their present unwillingness. And if you are backward to turn now, you are likely hereafter to be more averse when God is further departed from you, when Satan has built stronger holds in you, when conscience is grown more stupid, when custom in sin has doubled the strength and vehemence of your natural inclination to it. Alas! How many millions have died and been taken away in their iniquities that were as fully resolved upon repenting hereafter as any that are now alive? Take heed of this rock upon which so many have split and have been cast away forever. God's will is for the present. He says, *"Today if you will hear My voice, harden not your hearts,"* Heb.3:7-8. But if now, when God is

The Conversion of a Sinner

willing to give you life, you are unwilling, He may be hereafter unwilling when you would have it. When death and destruction come upon you as a whirlwind, He has threatened that you shall call upon Him for life and salvation, but it shall be far from you. *"You shall seek Him early, but you shall not find Him, if now you have knowledge, and do not choose the fear of the Lord,"* Prov.1:28-29.

C. A will upon a mistake is only a seeming will. Those whom our Lord likens to the stony ground heard the word with joy and were willing to embrace it, but they dreamed not of the cross and persecution. That made them fall away. Many seem willing to be converts, but they do not sit down and count the cost of conversion. And when once they are informed that they must deny themselves, let go of all their affections presently, and all their possessions, too, when they stand in competition with the Lord Jesus; when they are informed that a bill of divorce must be given to their Herodias, that they must bid defiance to every lust, though it pleads never so much delight or gain that it may still be embraced; when they are informed that they must watch and pray and walk with the greatest care, fervency, and circumspection; that they must take the Kingdom of Heaven with a holy violence, by storm, as it were, or else they will fall short and lose the crown, oh, then they cry out, *"These are hard sayings, who can hear them?"*

The Conversion of a Sinner

USE 3. Of exhortation. Since men die because they will, let me persuade you to consent that your wills may be renewed. Man has not a worse enemy than his own will until there is a change wrought in it. And that this change may be affection, observe these directions:

A. Judge yourselves because of your nature of perverseness. Until you are sensible of this, you cannot be humbled in a right manner. That you have sinned so much, so long, should very much affect and afflict you before God, but that you have a will to sin ten thousand times more, were it not for the restraints of grace, nay, to sin unto eternity, oh, what confusion and sorrow should this cause!

B. Study the deceitfulness of the tempter and the world. Then your hearts will not be so forward to be taken with their baits and to be drawn away from God. The world is vain and vexing, and Satan is a liar and a murderer. You have little reason to yield to either.

C. Set before your eyes the blessedness of life eternal and the misery of everlasting death that life may be chosen and the way to it.

D. Be fervent in prayers that the Lord, according to His promise, would give you a new heart and work in you to will of His own good pleasure, Ezek.36:26 and Phil.2:13. And if He causes your hearts to desire grace and glory, He will satisfy those desires He has raised in you. If He works in you to will and to do,

The Conversion of a Sinner

notwithstanding all opposition, you shall work out your own salvation, and an abundant entrance shall be administered to you in the everlasting kingdom. Thus of the second doctrine: The reason why men die, and die forever, is because they will.

DOCTRINE 3. The third doctrine follows. The Lord calls and calls again upon sinners to turn from their evil ways and live. *"Turn ye, turn ye,"* says God in the text. The business of conversion is not a thing which man first thought of. No, he would never think of it or be persuaded to it if the Lord did not call after him and make that call effectual. We read, indeed, in Scripture of sensible and awakened penitents crying and begging to be turned, but these cries are but, as it were, the echoes of God's voice and call that went before. In the handling of the doctrine, I shall first show how God calls upon sinners to turn to Him; secondly, why He does it; thirdly, explain the nature of this conversion or turning; and fourthly, conclude with application.

In the first place I am to show how God calls upon sinners to turn to Him. This He does in several ways.

1. He calls upon them from Mount Ebal. That was the Mount from whence the curses were denounced. He tells them in His Word of the cursedness and woe of the unconverted state. He sends the Law as a schoolmaster to teach them a sad lesson, that because of their frequent transgressions, they are just upon the

The Conversion of a Sinner

brink of eternal misery. And His design is that thereby they may be awakened and stopped in their destructive way and not flatter themselves with hopes of peace, though they still walk on after the imagination of their own heart.

This voice of the Lord by the Law is loud and terrible, uttered on purpose to rouse and startle them that are dead asleep. When the Law was delivered, *"there was a burning with fire, there was blackness, and darkness, and tempest, the sound of a trumpet, and the voice of words, which voice they that heard entreated that the word might not be spoken to them anymore, and so terrible was the sight that Moses said, I exceedingly fear and quake,"* Heb.12:18,19, 21. And if the manner of the Law's delivery was so dreadful, much more dreadful will be the manner of the Law's execution upon those by whom it has been violated. The fire and darkness at Mount Sinai were nothing in comparison with the fire of hell and the blackness of darkness there. Upon the impenitently wicked, the Lord has threatened *"to rain snares, fire and brimstone, and a horrible tempest, this shall be the portion of their trap,"* Ps.11:6. And truly this lecture of the Law is necessary that we may attain to a true knowledge and understanding of sin. And when we have been thus at the foot of Mount Ebal and Sinai, and have heard that sin is the great hindrance of all sorts of blessings and loads us with curses of all sorts,

The Conversion of a Sinner

both temporal and spiritual, and everlasting also, this is the way to cure our unreasonable doting upon it, and to make us fear and tremble because we have given so much way to it.

2. God calls upon sinners from Mount Gerizzim to turn to Him from whence of old the blessings were sounded forth. He not only gives them a sight of wrath as being nigh at hand while they continue to be workers of iniquity, but He also gives them a view of mercy afar off which shall be brought near to them on the condition that their wickedness is forsaken. Upon the righteous man's forsaking of his sinful ways and thoughts, mercy and abundant pardon are promised, Is.55:7. This call of the gospel from Mount Gerizzim is like the still voice after the strong wind, the fire, and the earthquake. How full of encouragement are those words in Zech.1:3, *"Turn unto Me, saith the Lord of Hosts, and I will turn unto you, saith the Lord of Hosts."* And Hosea 14:1, *"O Israel, turn unto the Lord thy God, for thou hast fallen by thy iniquity.* You have destroyed yourself, but in Me is your help found. I will heal your backslidings and will love you freely, though you deserve nothing but My anger and My hatred."

Satan, by tempting us to sin, has taken away our blessing from us, yet we ought not to despond for the Lord has more than one blessing. That which the first Adam forfeited, the second Adam was sent to restore,

The Conversion of a Sinner

Acts 3:26, *"God having raised up His Son Jesus, sent Him to bless you in turning every one of you from iniquity."* The Lord takes sinners up, as it were, into Mount Gerizzim. He shows them His kingdom and the glories of it. He tells them of His store of blessings, of the inestimable benefits which His Son has purchased: justification, adoption, sanctification, glory, and assures them that all shall be theirs if they will but turn indeed. And truly, these are other kinds of offers than Satan ever did or possibly can make.

3. God calls upon sinners to turn by the most passionate pleadings and pressing expostulations. His design in expostulating is to make them sensible of their unreasonableness in pursuing deceitful vanities, fulfilling their defiling lusts, and refusing to convert unto Him who can both sanctify them from their defilements and satisfy them with His all-sufficiency. He expostulates the matter with Judah, Is.55:2-3, *"Why will you spend your money for that which is not bread, and your labor for that which cannot satisfy?"* Since upon your coming to Me, the Life of your souls and the sure mercies of an everlasting covenant may be obtained."

The Lord pleads with the ungodly by the ministry of the Word after this manner: "What! Though you are told of sin's deceitful, defiling, and damnable nature, will you still embrace and hold it fast to My dishonor and your own destruction? Though you are

The Conversion of a Sinner

forewarned of the heat and heaviness of My anger, will you not flee from it? Though you are informed so often how little hell will be for your ease, will you run thither and burn there forever? Though you are told of a kingdom that cannot be moved, will not you be moved with desire after it, will you not be persuaded to strive for it? Are grace and glory of no worth at all? Is not a Saviour to be prized by them who, by sin, have enslaved and lost themselves, and are in danger of being lost unto eternity? Consider these things, and show yourselves men, oh, you transgressors." Thus the Lord pleads that He may prevail with sinners for their own good.

4. God calls upon sinners to turn by the example of others and by the voice of the rod upon themselves. The ungodly are very prone to observe bad examples that they may imitate them, but it is their duty to take notice when exemplary punishments are inflicted upon them that they may be afraid to follow them in wickedness any longer. When we behold others plagued for the sins of which we are guilty, the Lord bids us see the heinousness of our own iniquities in the strokes which others have felt before our eyes. And we may justly expect that like sins will have like ends if there is a continuance in provocation. Examples are purposely set before us *"that we may not lust after evil things,"* I Cor.10:6, that we may be admonished to turn out of these paths which have led others to ruin.

The Conversion of a Sinner

But especially when the rod falls upon our own backs, God calls upon us in a more perceivable and sensible way to turn to Him. The design of the rod is to embitter sin, both to the flesh and the conscience, that it may no longer be thought of as delightful, which is the procuring cause of every stripe that is endured. The rod has a voice as well as the Word, which it is our wisdom to hear. When affliction is laid upon the sinner's loins, by it the Lord speaks such language, Jer.2:17, *"Hast thou not procured this unto thyself* by sin? To turn from your iniquity is to consult your own ease; let the pain of the rod (which is yet nothing to the pains of hell) convince you that sin is not to be admired for its pleasure. At present you are only chastised with whips, but if you are incorrigible and sin ye more and more, assuredly at last you shall be lashed with scorpions."

5. God calls upon sinners to turn to Him by the internal voice and motions of His Spirit. The Spirit often suggests concerning the sinful and false way, "This is not the way, and therefore turn out of it." But concerning the way of holiness which leads to God, "This is the way, therefore turn unto it," and without declining, *"walk in it,"* Is.30:21. All the other calls will be to little purpose unless the Spirit accompanies them. Without His conviction, the denunciation of curses will not awaken. Without His illumination, the blessings proferred will be undervalued. Without His

-105-

The Conversion of a Sinner

setting an edge upon them, the most pathetical expostulations will not have the least efficacy to persuade. The loudest words will be no more regarded than if they were a whisper. Unless the Spirit joins His teaching and instruction, the rod will be mute and insignificant. Nothing will be learned, either by personal affliction or by national judgments. It is dangerous, therefore, to be heedless of, and resistant to, the Holy Ghost, since the efficacy of all depends upon Him.

There is a twofold call of the Spirit: more common and more special.

1. More common, and so many are called which never are thoroughly converted. It was the common work of the Spirit which made Felix tremble, which brought Agrippa within a step of Christianity and caused Herod to do many things. Multitudes of unregenerate ones have felt the waters stirred, the Holy Ghost moving them to conversion, and have readily proferred His aid and assistance, and perhaps, for awhile, they have been led by Him. But then they have refused to let go of some lust or vanity which He has bid them abandon. They would not turn their spiritual sloth into serious diligence about the concerns of their immortal souls, and so by disregarding His motions, and by slighting His help, they have made the Spirit to go away in grief who came in love to work upon them.

2. There is a call of the Spirit which is more special

The Conversion of a Sinner

and efficacious, and when He moves them to turn to God, sinners are not only almost, but altogether, persuaded. Now the method of the Spirit in working on those who are indeed made converts is much to be observed.

A. Those whom the Spirit calls effectually, He convinces of sin, John 16:8. He sets the Law before them, and He Himself is the Law interpreter. And by His commentary upon it, they are made to see that the Law forbids not only the breakings forth of sin at the lips and in the life, but also the inward lustings and risings of sin in the heart. And when the Law thus comes, oh! how does the offence abound! The Spirit sets their iniquities in order before their eyes and holds their eyes waking to behold them. The book of conscience is opened, and how many transgressions are presently beheld there registered? And if, upon dipping into this book, so many abominations appear, what an innumerable multitude are down in the book of God's remembrance? Though sinners may not consider it, yet God remembers all their wickedness, Hosea 7:2. This the soul lays to heart. *"Innumerable evils compass him about,"* says David, *"his iniquities take hold upon him,"* Psalm 40:12. When he lies down, they lie down. When he rises, they rise with him. Wherever he goes or is, they continually dog and haunt him.

If the sinner has been notorious, how hideous and

The Conversion of a Sinner

horrid will sin appear to him when all pleas and excuses are silenced, when the painted visor is pulled
off and it is seen by him in its native complexion?
Drunkenness, uncleanness, oaths, profane jesting, and
greediness after the world will no longer be made light
of. These and such like before seemed to have nothing
of danger, and much of delight and pleasure. But after
conviction, their deceitful and damnable nature will
be as evident as the sun at noon-day.

And though the sinner has been free from the more
gross pollutions of the world, yet enough shall be
shown him to cause him to conclude that he is a wretch
and in a lost estate. What! Are all his omissions or
mocking of the jealous God by heartless performance
nothing? Is his misspending of time and disregard for
eternity nothing? Is his delighting in creatures and
vanity, and the things of the world, and loving these
more than God and Christ and glory but a small
matter? These are heinous sins, which yet the more
civilized are to be charged with.

This conviction of the Spirit is strong and lasting.
It does not wear off until the sinner is brought quite
home. Actual transgressions with their aggravations
lie heavy, and original sin is the fountain whence the
other flow is discovered. And in this fountain, there is
enough to feed ten thousand times more streams than
have issued forth. David is not only convinced of the
murder and adultery he had committed, but is made to

trace these sins to the well-head, the original corruption of his nature, Ps.51:5. And the sight of this, how much did it tend to his humiliation?

Finally, this conviction is not only of some acts of sin, but of the badness of the sinner's estate. He is made to see himself, because he is a child of disobedience, as a child of wrath. Without cavilling, all is yielded to and acknowledged. With such evidence is the conviction of the Spirit.

B. Those whom the Spirit calls effectually, He works fear in them. The spirit of bondage to fear goes before the spirit of adoption. Of these fears and terrors there are degrees, indeed, yet such a measure is wrought in all towards whom the Lord has designs of love as to make them restless in a natural estate. Carnal security is one of the first things that is struck at by the Spirit. He bids the soul awake, and lets him know that while he sleeps in sin it is much more hazardous than if he slept upon the top of a mast.

Well may the sinner be afraid. He has engaged wrath armed with irresistible and almighty power against himself. *"And who can stand before God's indignation? Who can abide the fierceness of His anger?"* Nah.1. The curses of the Law have a dreadful sound in the sinner's ears, and, because threatened, damnation will not slumber long. The propinquity and nearness of such great evil raises fear exceedingly. His assent is strong, and in his mind he now foresees, *"the*

The Conversion of a Sinner

Lord Jesus revealed with His mighty angels in flaming fire, ready to take vengeance on them that know not God and disobey the Gospel, and to punish them with everlasting destruction," II Thess.1:8-9. And, oh, he thinks to himself, how terrible will it be to be of the number of them who shall call to the rocks and mountains to fall upon them that they may be hid from the face of Him that sits upon the throne and from the wrath of the Lamb! This causes him to make a halt in his wicked course. He dares not still rush into sin as the horse rushes into the battle.

C. Those whom the Spirit calls effectually, He raises grief and sorrow in them because of their sin and misery. They see what they have done against God and themselves, and this makes their spirits to be troubled. This is what being weary and heavy laden (of which the Scripture speaks) is in those whom Christ calls to come to Him that they may find rest unto their souls, Matt.11:28-29. There was a voice heard upon the high places, weeping and supplication of the children of Israel, because they had perverted their way and had forgotten the Lord their God, and this went before the closing with His invitation to return, John 3:21-22.

The sinner, by the Spirit, is made to behold the sadness of his case, the evil of sin, how miserably he has been deceived by his lusts and by Satan, and so his own folly in yielding to them. How does he now accuse and condemn himself? *"His heart is grieved,*

The Conversion of a Sinner

he is pricked in his reins, because he has been so ignorant and foolish, like a beast before God," Ps.73. He wishes a thousand times that temptations had been refused and that sin had never been committed.

I shall represent the working of the sinner's heart in this proposition: "Oh, wretched as I am, what have I been doing all my days! Was this the end that I was made for, to undo myself? Was there no better employment to be found than to add sin to sin, and so to treasure up wrath against the day of wrath? How much time have I misspent, and what pains have I taken to make myself miserable! Ah, foolish, self-destroying wretch! Do you not see how far you have provoked the Lord to anger? Oh, that my head were waters, and my eyes fountains of tears, that I might weep day and night! The damned will weep and wail forever, and shall I not mourn and weep who has so highly deserved to be damned? Well may I be troubled and bowed down greatly, and go mourning all the day long."

Thus the sinner grieves and bemoans himself, and carnal company, sensual pleasures, and worldly diversions cannot drive away this sorrow. None but He who broke the heart is able to bind up the wounds of it.

4. Those whom the Spirit calls effectually He causes to despair in themselves. They are made to perceive that they have no power in themselves out of those depths of sin and misery into which they have plunged themselves. And as they are unable to help

The Conversion of a Sinner

themselves, so they see that they are utterly unworthy to be helped. God may justly suffer them to lie where they are fallen, and, should He deal thus, they would fall lower and lower until they are fallen past recovery. The sinner may have recourse to his duties, hoping by these to make amends to God for what he has done amiss, but he is made to see that his best duties have so much sin mingled with them that, were it not for Christ's righteousness and intercession, they would be a mere abomination. Now he is beaten off from his own bottom. He has no confidence in the flesh, Phil.3:3. He can do nothing of himself. He can claim nothing as his due to be done for him, but he must be beholding to grace for all.

Upon this he cries out of the depths unto the Lord, Ps.130:1. He perceives himself as sinking and cries, "Lord, save me or I perish. I am at the brink of the bottomless pit, and I shall fall, unless the hand of mercy catches hold of me." He begs with Ephraim, "Turn Thou me, and I shall be turned." And as the evil of sin is presented to his view, so the goodness of God is, in some measure, by the Spirit revealed. And therefore, he desires to be converted, not only upon necessity, because else he would be extremely and eternally miserable, but also upon choice, because this is the way unto the truest happiness. And these desires to be turned are, as it were, the first breathings of the Spirit's operation in those whom He calls effectually

The Conversion of a Sinner

to turn to God, as also the several other ways how the Lord calls upon sinners to conversion, most whereof prove ineffectual, because those that are called are deaf, disobedient, and contrary.

My work, in the second place, will be to lay down the reasons why God does thus call the children of men to turn from their evil ways and live. The reasons are such as these:

1. Hereby He shows His gracious nature, that He delights not in the death and destruction of His creatures. Indeed, death will be inflicted upon them upon their obstinate continuance in evil, but showing mercy and giving life are the things that please God. Therefore He calls the most obdurate to conversion.

2. The Lord calls us to turn that hereby He may inform us of our duty. We may understand from hence that it is our duty to go astray no longer, but to come to our Father's house with speed. And by the pressing frequency of the calls, our obligation to this duty is vastly heightened. And truly the disregarding of our duty in this particular, and the great encouragements to it, our refusing to turn will do us more harm than all our sins. All other sins, upon our conversion, would be abundantly pardoned, but as long as we continue unconverted, not one is forgiven. The guilt of all lies upon us, and we assuredly lie under wrath.

3. The Lord calls upon us to turn to show that our

The Conversion of a Sinner

turning to Him will not be in vain. Though sin has very much abounded, yet there is not only a possibility, but a certainty upon our returning of our being graciously received and embraced. And this is a matter of great encouragement to a soul who lies under the apprehensions of sin and wrath. Hark what language is spoken unto Judah! Jer.3:1,5 -- *"Behold thou hast spoken and done evil things as thou couldst, thou hast played the harlot with many lovers; yet return again to Me, saith the Lord."* This call evidently shows that their transgressions, though multiplied exceedingly (if now they would but turn unfeignedly), should not be a bar to shut the doors of mercy against them.

4. The Lord calls upon us to turn to intimate that it is from Himself that we must have power and strength to turn in truth. The precepts and exhortations in Scripture to convert, to repent, to believe, and to stand fast and such are not delivered that from hence we might conclude that we have power in ourselves to do what we are commanded and exhorted to do, but they are delivered that we might turn these precepts into prayers. For instance, when we hear the command to believe, it should make us cry out with the sick child's father in the gospel, *"Lord, help my unbelief."* When we hear the command to cast away every transgression, it should make us beg with David, *"Order my steps in Thy word, and let not any iniquity have the dominion over me."* When we hear the command to turn, it should make us to use the language of the penitent, Jer.31:18, *"Turn Thou me and I shall be turned, for Thou art the Lord my God."*

5. The Lord calls upon us to turn to leave the obstinate without excuse who will not turn, who will not come to Christ that they might have life. Of Israel He said, *"All the day long have I stretched forth My hand to a disobedient and gainsaying people,"* Rom. 10, but their disobedience rendered them without apology. When the unconverted fall into God's revenging hands, they are the less to be pitied. They can have nothing to plead because God's stretching forth His hands by way of instruction in the gospel was in vain. These sinners against their own souls, whose neck is an iron sinew, who will neither be terrified by menaces nor mollified by the expressions of the greatest kindness and mercy, when they are summoned to the bar, how will they be struck speechless having not one word to say against their condemnation!

They were called unto grace and glory but they would not hearken. They were told of their danger but they would not seek to prevent it. They were informed of the ways of sin and were warned against them, nay, wooed and entreated with the most passionate earnestness not to be cruel to themselves by giving way to such a cursed thing, yet they would not be content to be freed from sin and become the servants of righteousness. And surely their mouths must be stopped,

The Conversion of a Sinner

or, if they say anything when sentence is passed upon them, it must be to side with the justice of God against themselves, to acknowledge the equality of His ways and the inequality of their own.

6. The Lord calls upon us to turn that those who are ordained to eternal life may be effectually worked upon and prevailed upon to turn indeed. We read that the gospel was preached both to the Jews and to the Gentiles, *"and as many as were ordained to eternal life believed,"* Acts 15:48. And the truth is, it is much for the sake of the elect who are scattered up and down among the multitude that the call is as general as it is. Hereby those whom the Father has given to Christ are brought home, and, coming home, how welcome are they? *"All that the Father giveth Me shall come to Me; and him that comes to Me, I will in no wise cast out."* So much for the reasons why God calls upon sinners to turn.

In the third place, I promised to explain the nature of this conversion or turning. And I find the Apostle gives a notable and full expression of it in Acts 26:18, where he calls it a turning from darkness unto light and from the power of Satan to God. Hence we gather that conversion lies in four things:

    1. In being turned from darkness;
    2. In being turned unto light;
    3. In being turned from the power of Satan;

The Conversion of a Sinner

4. In being turned unto God.

1. Conversion implies a being turned from darkness. As darkness was upon the face of the deep until God said, *"Let there be light,"* Gen.1:2, so truly darkness overspreads the soul of a natural man until he is enlightened from above. Believers are delivered from the power of darkness when they are translated into the Son's kingdom, Col.1:13. This shows that at some point they were in darkness as much as were others. And this darkness is said to have a power: a power to hold, a power to blind, a power to ruin, so that there is a necessity of being delivered from it. Now there are several kinds of darkness from which they are made free.

A. Converts are turned from the darkness of ignorance. No longer are they content to be ignorant of the way to salvation, but are made inquisitive as to what they must do to be saved. They are informed about the doctrine of Christ, and are made to understand what believing and repenting mean. They know that sin is to be sorrowed for as the worst of evils, and that God is the Chief Good, and that He *"so loved the world as to give His only begotten Son, that whosoever believes in Him should not perish but have everlasting life,"* John 3:16. They are made to know that Christ is to be received by faith, and that there is not salvation in any other, and that it is vain to expect anything from Him

The Conversion of a Sinner

as a Saviour unless there is a consenting to obey Him as a Lord. These and like truths are no longer hidden from them. They are sensible now of the mischief and danger of ignorance. It is therefore their desire to have it removed in a greater measure, and they follow on to know the Lord.

B. Converts are turned from the darkness of unbelief. The Spirit does a work of persuasion in their hearts of the certain truth of whatever God has revealed in His Word. They dare not make the Lord a liar any longer by not crediting what He has recorded. They believe and admire and acknowledge the mystery of God and of the Father and of Christ, Col.2:2. Heretofore, their unbelief hid the gospel from them and concluded them in a lost estate. They did not see the mystery of the Word. They were not taken with the treasures of wisdom and grace which are there revealed. Neither were they awakened by the terrors with which the Word abounds against ungodly ones. But now the veil is taken away, and they assent to, and are affected with, what the gospel speaks to them. They believe that God is in Christ reconciling the world to Himself, not imputing their trespasses against them, and that *"being justified by His blood, they shall be saved from wrath through Him,"* Rom.5:9. They believe that sin is deadly and the world a cheat, and that solid and eternal happiness is to be found in God. Therefore they leave a shadow to embrace that which

The Conversion of a Sinner

is substantial.

C. Converts are turned from the darkness of prejudice. Prejudice raises a strange kind of mist before the eyes which hinders the light of truth from shining into the mind. The Jews' prejudice against Christ was one great thing that blinded them, a principal impediment to their embracing the faith. Satan endeavored to fill the ungodly with these prejudices and to keep them up because by these his kingdom is very much upheld. Sometimes sinners are prejudiced against holiness as if it were a disgrace, whereas, being the glory of the Divine nature, certainly it is the greatest honor and perfection of which the rational creature is capable. Sometimes holiness is looked upon as needless and yet the Scripture affirms that none shall see the Lord without holiness. Sometimes the carnal heart rises against holiness because it imagines that nothing of delight and pleasure is consistent with it, whereas indeed by being converted unto God our joy is not lost, but only changed. The Kingdom of God is not only righteousness but also peace and joy in the Holy Ghost, Rom.14:17. The joy before was poor, low, brutish, and defiling, being mixed with many secret grudgings of conscience and misgivings of heart. Now upon conversion, the joy is pure, angelical, satisfying, and an earnest of those pleasures which shall be forevermore, Ps.16.

Neither is this unreasonable prejudice only against

The Conversion of a Sinner

the ways of holiness but also against the publishers of these ways. There was a prejudice against Elijah, as if he had been a troubler of Israel; against Jeremiah, as if he had been unfaithful to the state and a secret friend to the Chaldeans; against the Apostles, as if they had been intolerable disturbers who had turned the world upside down. And truly the treasure, oftentimes, is disregarded, though of such inestimable value, because of the vessel in which it is brought. But when any are turned, the mist of prejudice is immediately scattered. Then strict doctrine will go down which before was nauseating and made the heart to rise against it. Then a servant of Christ will be esteemed and obeyed who before was looked upon as the filth and off-scouring of the world, I Cor.4:13.

D. Converts are turned from the works of darkness. These works are cast off, Rom.13:12. No known presumptuous sin is allowed. They perceive the fruit-lessness of their former ways and therefore are ashamed of them, Rom.6:21. Formerly they went on securely in sin because they did not know where they were going, but now they perceive the tendency of these works of darkness, even unto blackness of darkness forever. And so they are made free from sin, that is from sin's servitude, and have become the servants of righteousness. Sin may plead hard against its being cast away, but all its pleas are invalid.

The gainful sin pleads thusly for itself, " I have

The Conversion of a Sinner

raised you from a mean to a high degree. I have filled your bag and furnished your table. By me you have gotten a fair estate who otherwise would have been only a little different than a beggar. And what, shall I now be cast off, having been so beneficial and having yielded so much advantage?"

But the convert has enough to reply to such a plea. Whatever he has gained unjustly he must restore. And if he had trusted in God and done good, he would have fared better. The mammon of unrighteousness is attended with a curse, and all the while he thrived in a wicked way, he was destitute of true riches. It is a wonder that by such dishonest gaining of the world he did not lose his soul long ago. Now, therefore, he is resolved against sinful gain lest, before he is aware, God and Christ and his soul are lost beyond recovery.

The pleasing sin is not without arguments for being cherished: "I have pleased your flesh and rejoiced your heart. I have made days and nights to pass insensibly away. I have gratified your senses and made your tongue to sing for joy. I have stupified and laid that fury called 'conscience' when it has begun to stir and torture you. I have chased away your cares and made you to forget your sorrows. Time was when the very thoughts of me were delightful and I was embraced as a darling. And why should I now be banished and killed as if I were an enemy? Is affliction of soul and brokenness of heart to be preferred before the

The Conversion of a Sinner

sweetness I was wont to afford you?"

But the convert's ear is deaf unto such a siren melody. One word is enough to dash and answer all, *"that the pleasures of sin are but for a season,"* Heb.11:25, but the pains of hell (which without conversion are sure to follow) will never have a period nor be in the least bit mitigated. The rich man who had lived lightheartedly and fared deliciously every day, when he was cast into the flames begged for just a drop of water and it was denied him. Therefore the works of darkness are cast off by the convert. The pleasure of these works is nothing compared to the pain, nor the gain to the loss which will speedily follow.

2. This conversion implies a being turned from darkness, so also a being turned unto light, Eph.5:8, *"for ye were sometimes darkness, but now are ye light in the Lord, walk as children of light."* And also II Cor.4:6, *"God Who commanded the light to shine out of darkness, hath shined into our hearts the light of the knowledge of the glory of God in the face of Jesus Christ."* This light has a threefold property: to reveal, to direct, and to operate.

A. This light reveals. The Apostle tells us, *"whatever makes manifest is light."* The convert sees what he never saw before. There may be many toads, serpents, and other loathsome and hateful creatures in a dungeon, but until the light shines in , these are not perceived. The breaking in of light reveals them. And

The Conversion of a Sinner

so in the heart of man many impure and offensive lusts have their abode, but they are not indeed acknowledged, neither are they any annoyance, until the light makes them manifest. The convert sees his sin, his shame. He is sensible of the plagues of his own heart and the absolute necessity of a cure. His interest, like-wise, is revealed to him, and that is in seeking first the Kingdom of God and His righteousness, in securing his soul which is of far greater value than the world, in minding the one thing needful, that good part which can never be taken away.

B. This light directs. It guides those who are turned into the way of peace and truth. The lamp of the Word (the Spirit joining with and teaching by it) shows which are the perverse and crooked paths to the end that these may be shunned and avoided. It also directs into those ways which are pleasing unto God and pleasant in themselves, and are, moreover, so exceedingly safe that no one ever missed heaven who continued to tread in them. We are directed to believe and obey, and where faith and obedience are linked together, the offspring of that conjunction will most certainly be glory, honor, and immortality.

C. This light operates in a powerful manner. It is such a light as has heat along with it. Converts were told before of the evil, of the folly of sin, but now they see this by another light and their hearts are warmed with indignation against it. They see sin so as to be

The Conversion of a Sinner

deeply affected. They sorrow for it and abhor it. They were informed before of the mercy and all-sufficiency and other perfections of God, but now they have such a view of His glory in the face of Christ that the fire of love is kindled and that love puts them upon labor.When Caleb had seen the good land of promise, he was very eager to go up at once and possess it, Num.13:30. And truly when this light has made a discovery of the celestial Canaan and directed converts how to get there, oh! what watching, what praying, what resisting, what striving, what storming will there be!

3. This conversion implies a being turned from the power of Satan. He is the spirit that works and rules in the children of disobedience, Eph.2:2, and has possession of them until converted. But then he is cast out and his strongholds are thrown down. And oh! Considering the devil's hatred, his power, his subtlety, what mercy is it to have the cords whereby he led us captive at his pleasure broken? Three things are comprehended in being turned from the power of Satan:

A. Those who are converted are freed from Satan's dominion. They have wisdom and grace to resist his usurped authority. The promise made to them who are not under the Law but under grace is that sin shall not have dominion over them, Rom.6:14. This necessarily implies that Satan's dominion shall be destroyed, for it is by the power of sin that he holds it. The net is now

The Conversion of a Sinner

broken and the soul escapes as a bird out of the snare of the fowler. The unconverted sinner, what a slave to Satan is he? If the devil tells him to go, he goes, no, he runs, though it is to his own ruin. The devil can only ask and have. The sinner's time and members, nay, and his soul, too, he can have upon demand. But the convert draws nigh to God, and is so strengthened by the grace of God that, instead of being commanded by Satan, he compels Satan to flee from him.

B. Those who are converted lay aside the work of Satan. They are aware of how base and injurious, both to God and to their own souls, the devil's employments are. And there is a better work than his, namely the work of the Lord which they labor in, and in the doing of which they cannot too much abound.

C. Satan's baits become despicable to those who are converted. It is by means of these that the devil is so powerful. The god of this world makes great use of this world to bewitch and ensnare the children of men. He exceedingly magnifies sensual delights, sumptuous fare, costly apparel, credit among men, and pleasant recreations. He suggests, " How happy these will make you!" He tells sinners of the worth of silver and gold, and often, through the burning-glasses of their eyes, he endeavors to set their hearts on fire by beauty. But the convert, by the eye of faith, looks higher than these things. He is made to see the vanity of the creature. He had impressions of divine displeasure,

The Conversion of a Sinner

and the world has appeared to him as an empty bubble, an insignificant cypher. His conscience was wounded, and when wounded, alas! It was not to be cured by any or all of the things the world could give him.

The convert was made to look upward and there perceives more durable riches, more lasting pleasure than the world can brag of. And so he is taken not with the things which are seen, but he is taken with the things which are not seen. Though he is in the world, yet he looks beyond it. Moses, having respect to the recompense of reward, refused to be called the son of Pharaoah's daughter, and slighted the pleasures of sin and all the treasures which were in Egypt.

4. This conversion, as it implies a being turned from the power of Satan, so it implies a being turned unto God. *" Turn unto Me,"* said the Lord of Hosts, *"and I will turn to you,"* Zech.1:3. As it is in a king's court, many that come there busy themselves in beholding the curious hangings and pictures which are there, but the wise statesman does not mind these things. His business is with the king himself. In like manner, while most of the creation is taken up wholly with the beholding, admiring, and pursuing this, that, and the other vanity, the convert (who shows himself herein to be truly wise) approaches and has recourse to God Who made these things, and can make him more happy than these are able to do.

Now when the sinner turns to God, he looks upon

The Conversion of a Sinner

Him under a threefold notion: as a Lord, as a Father, and as his Ultimate End.

A. The convert eyes God as a Lord. He owns His sovereignty and submits himself unto His scepter. Other lords have indeed in times past have had the dominion over him, Is.26:13, but now his resolution is fixed and peremptory to own no other Lord but God alone. His will stoops unto and complies with the will of God. When his natural inclination towards anything is most vehement, if the convert is informed that God by those things will be most displeased, that's enough to stop the current of his desires. He takes the testimonies of the Lord as a rule to order his conduct by, and when he hears that God has commanded him to keep His precepts diligently, his heart presently sends forth an echo back again unto that command, *"Oh, that my ways were directed, that I might keep Thy statutes!"* Ps.119:4-5. He dares not any longer presumptuously commit the evil which the Word forbids, nor omit the good which the Word commands.

Failings and infirmities there are and will be. *"In many things we offend all,"* said the Apostle, but this evil that is present with the convert is a burden to him. The Law of God is approved and consented to. It is delighted in as holy, just, and good. The convert (which distinguished him from a hypocrite) is far from wishing that the Law were less holy and that it would allow him liberty to sin, but he wishes that his heart

The Conversion of a Sinner

and life were more holy, and to the Law more and more conformable.

B. The convert eyes God as a Father, or as willing to become his Father in Jesus Christ. It was truly said by one of the Ancients, "None such a Father as God, none so full of fatherly affections." He has sufficient store to supply all the needs of the returning prodigals, and He is far more willing to impart of this store to them who see their need and ask than earthly parents can be to give bread unto their hungry children, Matt. 7:11. This is great encouragement to returning. Those parables of the lost sheep, the lost silver, and the lost son were uttered to this end: to hearten sinners to come home to God, Luke 15. The man rejoiced when he had found his sheep, the woman when she had recovered her piece of silver. That kind father, though necessity drove his child home, being ready to perish in the far country, and though he came home in rags having wasted all his substance in riotous living, I say that kind father, as soon as he saw his son, ran to him, had compassion on him, embraced him, kissed him, clothed him, adorned him, made a feast for him, and how glad he was that the lost child was found, that the dead son was alive again!

Surely we may conclude that God is willing to receive those that, being sensible that *"they have sinned and perverted that which is right, and it has not profited them,"* Job.33:27, return to Him with their

The Conversion of a Sinner

whole heart. It is true that the convert's sins and unbelieving heart together fill him many times with doubts and fears. He remembers God and is troubled because he has so bitterly provoked Him. He is afraid to call Him "Father" and very much doubts that he will be received. But then again faith and hope are encouraged by such promises as that which you read in II Cor.6:17-18, *"Touch not the unclean thing, and I will receive you, and I will be a Father unto you, and ye shall be My sons and daughters, saith the Lord Almighty."*

C. The convert eyes God as his Ultimate End. That God may be glorified, that God may be enjoyed is his design in turning. The sinner is sensible that while unconverted he lived to the dishonor of Him who gave him life, and in whose hand his breath is. Now, therefore, he has more zealous desires to walk worthy of the Lord unto all pleasing, being fruitful in those works which are unto His praise. Before, he sought himself, he sought his own things. He had no higher aim than to gratify his worldly and fleshly inclinations with what his carnal and corrupted mind judged to be suitable. He did not care how much the Lord was injured and provoked. But now he is of another mind. He carries on the same design that angels do, the same design that Christ did, namely, to honor and please the God of glory. And not only in his spiritual actions does he aim at this, but also in his

The Conversion of a Sinner

civil and natural actions, in his recreations, which hereby become spiritualized. He takes seriously what the Apostle said in I Cor.10:31, *"Whether therefore ye eat or drink, or whatever ye do, do all to the glory of God."* And now he lives like a creature, like a son. Before he lived like neither while he lived only to himself.

By thus glorifying God, the convert takes the right course to enjoy Him. He looks upon God as the best portion and therefore pitches upon Him. This is now his language: "Let the men of the world take the things of the world if they please. Let them pursue after bubbles. Let them toil and vex themselves for that which, when gotten, will prove only a further vexation. My soul seeks after God. He alone deserves my seeking. He alone, when found, can satisfy me to the uttermost."

Nothing short of God will content the convert. Wealth cannot do it. Credit, sensual delights cannot do it. No, ordinances themselves are but like empty breasts and broken cisterns unless communion with God is enjoyed in them. He prays for God, he hears for God, he fasts for God, he comes to the table for God. Earth is like hell when God is absent, and he judges that heaven would not be heaven if God were not always present. Thus I have showed wherein conversion lies, in being turned from darkness to light, and from the power of Satan to God.

The Conversion of a Sinner

I shall add a word or two further to manifest through whom it is that sinners must turn to God if they would be received. And the truth is, it is through Christ alone. The Apostle plainly affirms *"that through Him both Jews and Gentiles have access by one Spirit unto the Father,"* Eph.2:18. And our Lord, in expressed terms, says in John 14:6, *"I am the way, the truth, and the life; no man cometh unto the Father but by Me."* It is impossible that such guilty and polluted creatures as we have made ourselves by sin should ever be accepted before a just and holy God without a Mediator. Hence it follows that there is a necessity we should look unto Jesus, to use the Apostle's phrase, *"in Whom God is reconciling the world unto Himself,"* II Cor. 5:19. Otherwise, we should not dare to approach, but fly away for fear of being (as we deserve to be) consumed.

Now when we look unto Jesus the Mediator, we must look upon Him as our Righteousness, as our Advocate, and as our Helper.

1. We must look upon Christ as our Righteousness. This is the name whereby that branch that springs from David is called, *"The Lord our Righteousness,"* Jer. 24:6. There is no coming unto God without some righteousness or another. Our own righteousness is like filthy rags, and because it is rags it is not able to cover us; because it is filthy rags it cannot adorn or commend us. Therefore, we must look unto Jesus to be

The Conversion of a Sinner

made righteousness to us that, for the sake of His obedience and suffering in our stead, our sins may be forgiven and our persons may be accepted in the sight of God. The righteousness of Christ which is imputed to believers is in every way perfect and sufficient, so that the pure and piercing eye of God cannot spy the least flaw or defect in it. If therefore we are covered with this, none of our sins will appear against us or be laid to our charge. Christ has died and, upon His death, God justifies. Who, therefore, shall accuse or condemn those that believe?

2. When we turn to God we must look upon Christ as our Advocate, I John 2:1, *"If any man sin , we have an Advocate with the Father, Jesus Christ the Righteous."* This Advocate, as He suffered to purchase pardon and grace, so He interecedes that these may be bestowed upon returning sinners, and God His Father always hears Him. We ought to consider, and to be encouraged by considering, what a High Priest we have at the right hand of God. When the sinner beholds himself, in himself undone, and comes petitioning for remission of sin, for the healing of his spiritual plagues, and for the saving of his soul, which seems to be just upon the borders of damnation, this Advocate will take the sinner's petition and present it to His Father, and all shall be granted, aye, and infinitely more than the sinner can desire or conceive.

3. When we turn to God we must look upon Christ

The Conversion of a Sinner

as our Helper. He strengthens the feeble knees, otherwise we would not be able to set one step in the way to life. The Lord Jesus is called *"the Author of our faith,"* Heb.12:2, and by Him believers are said to have access into that grace wherein they stand, Rom. 5:2. The sinner must be made sensible of his own insufficiency to turn himself, to set himself at liberty, and upon this must look unto the Son of God to bring his soul out of prison, to make him free indeed from the curse of the Law, from the bondage of corruption, and to enable us to come to God and cleave to Him.

In the last place follows the application.

USE 1. OF EXAMINATION

Since God calls upon sinners again and again to turn, it highly concerns all to examine whether this call has been obeyed! It is wisdom to bring our grace to the Touch-stone since there is so much counterfeit grace in the world. As it is easy and common to mistake in this matter, so there is no mistake more dangerous, and it won't be long before it will be impossible to correct mistakes about salvation. The damned see wherein they deceived themselves, but alas! It is now too late to think of turning better. The door to mercy is shut and barred, and will be barred forever. I remember Theodoret, commenting upon this text, observing that the doubling of the words *"turn ye, turn ye,"* gives us

The Conversion of a Sinner

to understand the sincerity which is required in conversion. A bare appearance sets us at a farther distance from God.

Here I shall speak of some changes that have a kind of likeness to conversion, which yet are to be found in them that fall short both of grace and glory.

1. Those cannot be said to be converted who are only turned to such or such a party or opinion about smaller matters in religion. Suppose your opinion is orthodox and right. What's that if your heart is not right in the sight of God? Those who please themselves because they have the name of Non-Conformists, what does this signify unless they refuse to conform to the sinful fashions and courses of the world? On the other side, they that boast of being sons of the church, what advantage will that be if by their swearing, lying, and hatred of holiness they show themselves to be the sons of Belial?

2. Those are not converted whose turning is only partial. Saul obeyed the command of the Lord in part against Amalek. That which was vile and refuse he utterly destroyed, but delicate Agag and the best of the spoil he spared, I Sam.15:9. This partial obedience is censured as high rebellion in verse 23. Many will yield to God's call in some degree. They will consent to mortify the sins which they can easily spare, but the chief, the darling, the delicate sin which they live, or live so sweetly with, that shall not be touched!

The Conversion of a Sinner

Herod was a partial convert. In sundry respects he yielded obedience to the Baptist's preaching, but when John would have turned him from his incest with Herodias, this could not be borne. Instead of obeying the message, he persecutes, and later kills, the messenger.

3. Those are not converted who only turn to God in the time of their extremity and afterwards are guilty of revolting. Israel, when Sinai was all in a fire before their eyes, turned to God for fear of being consumed. Then they cry out that they *"will hearken and do whatever the Lord should speak to them,"* Deut.5:27. But before a few days were expired, they quickly turned out of the way which God commanded them and fell into gross idolatry. And again we read, *"when God slew them when they fought Him, they returned and inquired after Him; and yet all this while their heart was not right, neither were they steadfast in His covenant,"* Ps.78:34-37. How many sick-bed resolutions have looked like conversions which, upon the return of health, have vanished quite away? True conversion is a lasting change. There may indeed be falling fits and fits of slumber, *"The wise virgins slumbered and slept,"* Matt.25, though they were not overly wise to do so, but yet true converts never go so far as to change their Lord and choose anything but God for their Chief Happiness.

Reader, beware of being only almost a convert, as

The Conversion of a Sinner

you would be unwilling to be only almost saved and quite damned.

The question now will be, how may true conversion be discerned from all those shows whereby multitudes are deluded? Unto this I answer in these particulars.

1. In true conversion the heart is turned from the love of every known iniquity. The strength of sin lies in the love of it, and love to it plainly argues that it holds the heart in its possession still. The convert's language is this: "I esteem Your commands concerning all things to be right and I hate every false way," Ps.119:128. Your love is that which God principally requires of you. If sin, if the world runs away with that, how can you have the nerve to say you are turned? It is not sufficient to abstain from the outward act of sin, a hypocritical Pharisee may go that far, but the very soul must abhor it. Especially the sin that has been most desired, most delighted in, will be most detested when conversion is sincere. The covetous man, when turned, will most abhor covetousness; the unclean, their filthiness; the proud, their pride; and the reason is evident, because by these sins God has been most displeased and dishonored, and they, most of all, have been polluted and defiled.

2. In true conversion, there is a renewing of the whole man. All things are become new, says the

The Conversion of a Sinner

Apostle in II Cor.5, in them that are new creatures. Old things are passed away. The whole man is sanctified, though not wholly sanctified. Every part is changed, though the change is not perfect. The understanding is enlightened, the conscience is made tender and has a great command. The heart makes choice of God and desires His favor and fellowship. The members are yielded as instruments of righteousness unto holiness. The convert willingly resigns and gives up his whole self, both body and spirit, to the Lord.

3. In true conversion, there is a desire to be turned more and more. There is a hungering after a greater degree of righteousness. The remainders of flesh are a burden, and *"the Spirit lusts against them,"* Gal.5:17. The convert goes to God to perfect that which concerns him, to strengthen what He has worked for him. "Lord, You have done much for me, but there is much more still to do. There are many enemies still to slay, many distempers still to heal, many spots still to wash out, many wrinkles still to smooth. Oh! You who have laid the foundation, rear up the building and at last bring forth the top stone, that I may cry, 'Grace, grace, forever!' "

4. In true conversion, there is a pure and fervent love to converts. Love to the brethren is a sign of being passed from death to life, I John 3:14. Let them be lowly, poor, of weak parts, let them be villified and despised by the world, yet if they are saints they will

The Conversion of a Sinner

be esteemed and owned by them that are sincerely changed. Then our love is right when the more holy any are, the more we love them and the more holy designs they have upon us. The more plainly they deal with us for the sin which they see in us, still we affect them the more ardently. Yea, and we can rejoice in their grace, though because of their luster we shine more obscurely.

5. In true conversion, there is a pity toward the unconverted. Those who are turned have escaped danger and they cannot but be moved with other's peril. How can they do anything but mourn over their relations and acquaintances that are without Christ in the world? Oh, what hazard do they run? When they go to sleep, they do not know but that they may wake in the midst of flames that are unquenchable! When they go out of their houses they may be in hell before they return! They hang over the bottomless pit by the small thread of their lives and a thousand things may happen every day which are sufficient to break that thread asunder. Then in they fall without redemption.

Oh, doleful state of the ungodly! If you who are a religious wife should wake in the night and find your husband stone dead by you, would it not extremely amaze and grieve you? Oh, if you who are the master of a family should all of a sudden find all your children and servants dead before your eyes, would not your heart be extremely affected? And surely if your

The Conversion of a Sinner

husband, your wife, your children, your servants are dead in sins, in danger of being damned forever, you have much more reason to be concerned for them and to endeavor by advice and prayers and tears to have them turned and reconciled to God.

Now reader, try yourself by these signs of conversion. If you find them in yourself, you may rejoice for these plainly show that your name is written in the Book of Life. But if any sin is loved, your mind and conscience, your heart and life, are all defiled. And as you are unrenewed, so you have no desire after renewing grace. If you delight in the carnal and are a hater of saints, this shows that you are a stranger to conversion and are in the gall of bitterness to this hour.

USE 2. OF TERROR

Whoever you are, high or low, rich or poor, male or female, who reads these lines and was never turned, I am sent to you from God with heavy tidings such as, if you were not a brute or a stock, would make you like Belshazzar, when upon the view of the handwriting upon the wall, *"his countenance was changed, his thoughts troubled him, the joints of his loins were loosed, and his knees smote one against another,"* Dan.5:6. I am not going to prophecy good concerning you, but evil. I have a roll to deliver to you, but it is

The Conversion of a Sinner

written within and without with lamentation, murmuring, and woe. You are, perhaps, jolly and secure, but this is like the mirth and laughter of a sick man who is out of his senses, which argues his distemper to be all the sorer. Alas! Sinner, you do not have reason to smile while you are in a state of nature. How many threatenings are denounced against you? And suppose you were surrounded with cannons, all ready at once to be discharged at you. These would be nothing near as dreadful as the threatenings and curses which the just and jealous God has uttered. Open your eyes and look whichever way you will. Enough may be perceived to cause your heart to meditate on terror; above, an angry God; below, a flaming hell; behind, an innumerable host of sins pursuing you; before, Satan and the world leading you along in the broad way to destruction.

But more particularly, I would have these following truths laid to your heart:

1. While you are unconverted, you are also unpardoned. You stand indebted for many thousands of talents, and not so much as one mite of all that debt is paid. The least transgression makes you liable to the curse of the Law, and guess then what an accursed wretch your many and your mighty sins have made you? Upon your returning and acknowledging of your iniquity, God has engaged to do it away. He will lay the load on the back of a Mediator, but, if you will not

The Conversion of a Sinner

consent to be turned, you alone must bear it. Sin is another kind of thing than you imagine. Adam's first transgression in eating the forbidden fruit (which was aggravated because he would have been as God, and he believed the serpent and made God a liar, and which was, indeed, a rejecting of the whole Covenant of life made with him), oh! how it made him to smart! And not only himself, but his whole progeny are the worse for it. And if one sin has brought a curse upon all the children of men, think, O soul, how will you be able to stand under all the sins you have committed? Sin makes the whole creation groan, it makes the damned to lament and to despair and will be an intolerable load forever.

Sin was found heavy by our Lord. This caused His anguish and made His soul exceedingly sorrowful, even unto death. Nay, God Himself complains that He is pressed with iniquity. A cart is pressed which is full of sheaves, and will you, sinner, make light of it? Oh! How heavy will you one day feel it!

2. While unconverted, you are treasuring up more and more wrath against the day of wrath. Your scores are large already, but every day you run up the score afresh. Every day you make new wounds, though conscience now is so stupid that it feels nothing. As your skin abounds, proportionably, the vials of Divine indignation grow fuller, which will at last be all emptied upon your head. It is unnatural cruelty to be

The Conversion of a Sinner

a devil to yourself, to be your own soul's murderer! You are continually setting yourself at a greater distance from God and engaging Him more and more against you, who alone can be a Refuge and Salvation to you. You will perceive at last that you have been your own foe and acted to your own confusion. Jer.7:19, *"Do they provoke Me to anger, saith the Lord, do they not provoke themselves to the confusion of their own faces?"*

3. While unconverted, you render yourself more and more unfit for glory and blessedness. The more impure you are, the more unfit you are to see God. The abominations which are loved and wrought by you make an improper inhabitant for the new Jerusalem. The inheritance above is an inheritance of saints. It is an incorruptible and undefiled inheritance, I Pet.1:4. The company is all holy and so are the employments.There is not a vain or sinful word spoken there, nor an impure desire or thought to be found in any that are above. And what would you do there among them unless a change is worked in you?

4. If you do not turn, you are sure to die. As life is far off, so death is near. The Psalmist tells us that *"God is angry with the wicked every day, and if he turn not, He hath whet His sword, He hath bent His bow and made it ready,"* Ps.7:11-12. And when the instruments of death are thus prepared, it is a sign that God will make quick work and suddenly cut the offender

The Conversion of a Sinner

off. Death is called a "King of Terrors," and it well deserves that name in respect of the ungodly. Then their good things are all received and their evils come upon them which will never be removed. Their torments begin which will never know an end. As long as God is God, they have God for their enemy. As long as God is happy, they will lie in the most extreme misery! What tongue can utter or heart imagine the horror of this? An angry, sin-revenging Lord will lay your load upon you, and yet will keep you from sinking into nothing. He will uphold you in your being that you may be plagued forever. He will show His mighty power in holding you up with one hand that He may lash you with the other unto all eternity.

USE 3. OF CONSOLATION

You who have obeyed the call of God to turn, I am commanded to speak peace and comfort to you, Is. 40:1, *"Comfort ye, comfort ye My people, saith your God."* The unconverted are not more accursed than you are blessed. I have several things to tell you which are enough to make your hearts leap for joy.

1. God has had thought of love towards you from before the foundation of the world was laid. He predestinated and chose you unto the adoption of children, Eph.1, long before you were. From everlasting He

The Conversion of a Sinner

designed to make you heirs, and joint-heirs with Christ unto that kingdom and glory with which the sufferings of this present time are not worthy to be compared. And since the love of God towards you is from everlasting, is co-eternal with Himself, it can never in time be changed.

2. God has justified you freely by His grace through the redemption of Jesus Christ, Rom.3:24. *"As far as the East is from the West, so far are your iniquities removed from you,"* Ps.103:12. And surely that's as far as you can desire. They are cast into the depth of the sea, which argues that when they come to be sought for they shall not be found, just as those things which are cast into the depth of the sea, we despair that they should ever be recovered. *"Christ has been wounded for your transgressions, He has been bruised for your iniquities,"* Is.53:5. And as the imputation of your sins to Christ caused Him to undergo real sufferings, so the imputation of His righteousness to you will cause a real exemption from that wrath and punishment which, by sin, you have justly merited. Be of good cheer, converts, your sins are forgiven and, consequently, the curse of afflictions and also the sting of death is taken away.

3. You that are converts, it won't be long before you are glorified, Rom.8:30, *"Moreover, whom He did predestinate them He also called, and whom He called them He also justified, and whom He justified*

The Conversion of a Sinner

them He also glorified." The Lord has promised that
those who overcome shall sit with Him on His throne.
You shall not only overcome, but be more than con-
querors through Him who has loved you. Mansions
are already prepared for you, and when you are prepared for those mansions, you shall be received unto
them. Then neither the fury nor the favor of the world
will be a temptation. Satan's fiery darts will not be able
to reach you when you are gotten into the third
heaven. When you are just entering into the new
Jerusalem, you will shake hands with both sin and
misery at the door, and neither of them will be able to
follow. Tears will be wiped away and the cause of
sorrow will be gone. There will be a clear view of God
without the least cloud. The Sun of Righteousness will
shine forever without any eclipse. There will be entire
joy without grief, perfect peace without any trouble,
complete holiness without the least remainder of corruption, a full blessedness without period.

USE 4. OF EXHORTATION

And who would not now become a convert? Have
you anything to say against a pardon or against that
glory which has been revealed? Shall it be made a
question, whether pleasure forever more or eternal
torments are to be preferred? Oh, that you would come

The Conversion of a Sinner

to yourselves! And then I am sure you would come to God immediately. The arguments to persuade you to conversion are divers.

1. If you turn not, you cannot answer the end of your creation. You must not think God gave you a being and sent you into the world to please yourselves, to satisfy your inordinate and corrupt desires, and to live carelessly and rebelliously against Him. But thus you do until you are converted. Did the Lord give you an understanding faculty, and not design that He should be understood and known by you? Did He give you a heart to love and to desire, and not design Himself as the Chief Object of both? Did He give you affections that you should give them away to sin and vanity? Oh, do not cross the end for which you were made any longer lest you cause the Lord to *"repent and grieve at the heart He made you,"* Gen.6:6, and so resolve to destroy the workmanship of His own hands. If you continue obstinate and without understanding, *"He that made you will not save you, or have mercy on you; He that formed you will show you no favor,"* Is.27:11.

2. Unless you turn, you cannot answer the end of the death of Christ and the redemption wrought thereby. Our Lord did not die only to expiate offenses, but also to purify unto Himself a peculiar people, zealous of good works, and that *"in the body of the flesh, through death, He might present them holy and*

The Conversion of a Sinner

unblameable," Col.1:22. *"Through the eternal Spirit, He offered up Himself without spot to God, that by His blood He might purge our consciences from dead works, to serve the living God,"* Heb.9:14. From these and other similar places, it evidently follows that not only our pardon but our purity was designed by the Lord Jesus. But how can we be pure unless we turn to God from sin which defiles us? Christ knew what a sickness and debasement of our nature sin is, therefore He Himself was slain that sin might be killed. And will you dare to live in sin? Hark to the Apostle in I Pet.2:24, *"Who His own self bore our sins in His body on the tree, that we, being dead to sins, should live unto righteousness, by whose stripes ye were healed."* And as the death of Christ is an argument to persuade us to turn from sin, so from this death, virtue and power is now to be derived whereby sin may be subdued.

3. You are further obliged to turn because of God's condescension in giving you leave to do it. If the gulf had been fixed upon the very first transgression, if the turning of fallen man had been as impossible as the turning of fallen angels, the Lord could not have been charged with the least injustice. But although you have departed, He calls after you. Without any detriment or prejudice to His justice, He has found a way to show you mercy. The devils were never called to conversion. As soon as they had sinned, they were fettered in chains of darkness that shall never be unloosed. But

The Conversion of a Sinner

hark what wisdom says, Prov.8:4, *"Unto you, O man, I call, and My vow is to the sons of man."* You have often stopped your ears. Oh, that at last you would hear that your souls may live. The long deafening of your ears may provoke the Lord to shut His mouth and then you will never be converted, never healed.

4. Consider who it is that calls upon you to turn and what is His design in it. You are undone wretches who have neither skill, nor will, nor power to save yourselves. And He that calls after you is a God to whom power and mercy belongs, and His design is to make His power and mercy known to you. His aim is to bring you near that He might manifest Himself to you as He manifests Himself unto the world, to shield you from danger, to supply your needs according to the riches of His glory, to deliver you from every evil work, and to preserve you to His heavenly kingdom, and is there any harm in all of this?

5. It is unreasonable that the world or sin should be a hindrance and should stave you off from God any longer. Well you may turn from sin, for that deserves your hatred. Well may your hearts turn from idolizing the world and the things of it, for these deserve your scorn. All things besides God are either hurtful or helpless. Nothing is more hurtful than sin, and they that have expected help from the creatures have found themselves destitute and forlorn in their extremity.

6. If you turn to God, He will not fail to turn to you.

The Conversion of a Sinner

His ear shall be turned and shall be open to your cry. His hand shall be upon you for good, and in the hollow of His hand you shall be secure. He is greater than all, and none is able to pluck you out of His hands. He will not hide, but turn His face towards you. He will give you peace as well as mercy. He will let you know that pardon is multiplied that your love also may be increased. The debtor loved much to whom much was forgiven. Finally, the stream of His benefits shall be turned towards you. The Lord will do you good and delight in doing so. Temporal things you shall not want. Spiritual blessings shall be showered down abundantly, and at last you shall ascend and be admitted into His immediate presence where God will turn to you so as never to withdraw again. Be not afraid or dismayed, whoever turns against you for conversion's sake. The Lord Himself is with you and for you, and He will turn to good what adversaries mean for evil.

7. Not only His Word and ministers and Spirit, but also His providences call upon you to turn to God. Both His mercies and His judgments press this exhortation to conversion. The streams of goodness that continually run towards you, and which sometimes swell and overflow abundantly, signify that it is your wisdom to forsake the broken cisterns and come to the fountain of living waters. His mercies speak this language, that it is good to return to, and obtain an

The Conversion of a Sinner

interest in, the Father of them. Then these mercies will be in mercy. Cords of love are cast about you on purpose to draw you unto the God of love and peace. Oh, that you would run to Him! The riches of His goodness are unlocked and discovered that hereby you may be led unto repentance, Rom.2:4.

His judgments, likewise, are inflicted in pursuance of the same design. That is the voice that's uttered by them, *"Go return unto the Lord, for He hath torn and He will heal you; He hath smitten, and He will bind you up,"* Hos.6:1. The fire of London calls upon the inhabitants of it, and of the whole land (since they have not only heard of God by the hearing of the ear, but their eyes have seen Him marching out so dreadfully against them), to abhor themselves and to repent in dust and ashes. Those many thousands that were cut off by the plague of pestilence, although they are dead, they still speak, and that which they say is this, "Oh, you who are alive, return unto the Lord your God, for after death it will be too late to do it."

8. Consider, as yet it is not too late to return to God. Though hitherto stupid, if now you will awake; though hitherto refractory, if now you will yield yourselves to the Lord; though hitherto you have shut the door to keep sin in and to keep Christ out, if now at last you will open at the knock of the gospel and consent that your lusts should be expelled and the Lord Jesus enter, He is ready to receive you into grace

The Conversion of a Sinner

and favor, and all former denials, affronts, and re-pulses shall be forgotten and forgiven. The scepter is still held forth, the Lord is not removed from His mercy-seat. Mercy and grace may now be had if you will come for it. But if you will not know when you are well-offered, and are resolved not to cease from your stubborn way, an oath may soon be sworn in wrath that you shall never enter into rest. God may say, "He that is filthy, let him be filthy still. He that is unjust, let him be unjust still. He that is joined to the profits and pleasures of the world which he makes his idols, let him alone. He that despises the offer of grace shall not have another offer; he who now refuses to be con-verted shall never be a convert."

Oh, that I could prevail by all these arguments. But lest they should take no impression, lest they should slip out of your minds and have no influence upon your hearts, I shall second them:

1. With a voice from hell;
2. With a voice from heaven;
3. With a voice from Christ Himself.

1. With a voice from hell. Imagine, therefore, a damned sinner who has lain many years in the burn-ing lake. Suppose he should have leave to come and appear in the face of this assembly, and a river of tears having gushed out of his eyes, and for awhile he

The Conversion of a Sinner

stopped his expressions, he at length should thus speak to you:

"Cursed be the day wherein I was born, and that night wherein it was said that there is a manchild conceived! Let that day be darkness, let not God regard it from on high, neither let the light shine upon it. Alas, it were better never to have been at all than to be forever miserable! How intolerable are the gnawings of the never-dying worm? How hot and unquenchable are those flames which the breath of the Lord as a stream of brimstone kindles?

"The world is extremely mistaken in sin. They think it light and pleasant, and so I once thought it as well as they. But now I find how woefully I was deceived. I feel sin's weight and taste, yea, I am drunk with the gall and wormwood of it. I find that true which before I was told but would not believe, that it is a fearful thing to fall into the hands of the living God. His mighty hands have taken hold of me and bound me hand and foot and thrown me into outer darkness. And there I must lie tortured to eternity! Oh, that word rends my very heart, kills all hope, sinks and quite overwhelms me in utter desperation.

"If after millions of millions of ages my torments were to end, I should strengthen myself under my sorrows, but since after so long a space of time I shall be as far from releasing as the first moment I was imprisoned, this is that which makes my grief to know no bounds, because misery knows none. Oh, what frenzy possessed me that for the sake of a little gain and pleasure for a short season which sin yielded me, I should venture to dwell with devouring fire, and to inhabit everlasting burnings!

"But I must only blame myself. God is severe, but not in the least unrighteous. He called, but I refused. He stretched forth His hand, but I disregarded Him. I set at nought all His counsel and would have none of His reproofs. I remember very well that He spoke to me often to turn out of the paths that lead to destruction and misery, but I would still go on. I was warned to flee from the wrath to come, but I would not take any warning. I was entreated to be reconciled, but resolved to continue a rebel. I would not be made clean though the Lord waited to be gracious!

"And what! Will any of you continue in the same desperate mind that I was of? Will you still cherish the self-same sins that were my undoing? Behold the flames about my ears. Oh, that you could conceive the anguish of my heart! Be wise, be wise, and accept mercy and salvation while it is tendered to you, for if once you come to this place of torment, the Lord will forget to be gracious, and His mercy will be quite and clean gone forever!"

2. A voice from heaven. Suppose one of the glorified saints who has been an inhabitant of the heavenly Jerusalem, who has conversed with an innumerable

The Conversion of a Sinner

company of angels and has seen God face to face, should, for awhile, leave his blissful mansion and having abundance of joy and glory in his looks should utter such language as this before you:

"Oh, the height, and length , and depth, and breadth of the love of Christ which passes knowledge! How unsearchable is His goodness, and His mercy past finding out! Worthy is the Lamb that was slain to receive power, and riches, and wisdom, and strength, and honor, and glory, and blessing, for by His blood He has redeemed me, with millions more out of every kindred, tongue, people, and nation! I was called to turn and live, and through rich grace was enabled to obey the call. And now I find what a glorious life that is unto which sincere and persevering converts shall at last be brought. This is a life that's free from sin and free from suffering, that will never see death or be in danger of the grave.

"It is best of all to be near to God. Christ is without all controversy the best Master. To be subject to Him is to reign and reign forever! What ails the blind and stupid world that they see no form nor comeliness in this fairest among ten thousand, the light of whose countenance makes heaven not to need the light of the sun, moon, or stars! His beauty is all-surpassing, His grace is much more than gold that perishes, but His glory, it is not lawful or possible for me to utter.

"And now, will any of you slight Him any longer?

The Conversion of a Sinner

Open your eyes and see evidently that you are the children of perdition, the sons of death without Him. But through Him you may be turned. Through Him you may be saved with a great and everlasting salvation. Surely, then, you have reason to value Him above all, though the whole world, nay, though ten thousand worlds should stand in competition with Him."

3. Hear a voice from Christ Himself. Imagine the Lord Jesus appearing with a light from above the brightness of the sun. Suppose some of His angels as harbingers and forerunners came before Him and cried out, *"Holy, holy, holy, is the Lord of Hosts,"* and at last Himself visibly filling this place with His majesty and His glory. And, having stricken awe into you, and having wrought in you an admiration for His excellency and greatness, suppose that He spoke thus to you:

"Look unto Me and be saved, all you ends of the earth. I am your Redeemer, and there is none else. You have destroyed yourselves, but in Me and Me alone you may find help. Unless I make you free, sin will still reign in you, and if it reigns, it will also ruin. Unless I bind the strong man armed, he will keep you bound and lead you captive at his pleasure. Unless I turn and bring you near to God, you will run farther and farther away from Him until at last there is no possibility of returning. How long, you simple souls, will you love

The Conversion of a Sinner

simplicity, and you fools hate knowledge? Turn at My reproof. Behold, I will pour out My Spirit upon you. I will make known My words unto you.

"Former contempts I will pass by if now at last you will receive Me. I will free you from the guilt and power of sin. I will pacify My Father's anger, though by breaking His laws and despising Me, His Son, you have never so much incensed Him. Though by nature captives, I will make you kings and priests. Though by sin traitors and enemies, I will make you sons and heirs of God and co-heirs with Myself, who is the Heir of all things. You shall in no case be miserable, if all the fullness which dwells in Me can satisfy you and make you happy."

And after all this, my brethren, will you be fond of sin and ruin? Oh, hear the voice of the Son of God, who is not willing that you should perish. What shall I do to work on you? I think that I would be willing that these words should be my last, upon the condition that they might be powerful and effectual to the converting, healing, and saving of all that are within the sound of them. I think that I could be willing to expire here and be carried dead out of the pulpit upon the condition that all you might hear so as to turn from your evil ways and live.

Most of those thousands which are before me are unknown to me, but this I know, that you have souls and that every soul is worth a world. Oh, that you all would consult your soul's interest and safety!

But lest it should be in vain if I only speak to you, I shall direct my words to Him who is Lord over all:

"And oh, that He who works, and none can let or hinder, would work a thorough, saving change in you! Oh, that He would pity those among you who are cruel unto yourselves! Oh, that He would awaken the souls that are not only asleep, but dead! And break the hearts which have made themselves an adamant stone! Oh, that He would convince you of your sin and misery, and effectually turn you from the one, that you may be freed forever from the other!"

To these petitions, let every heart say, "**AMEN!**"

USE 5. OF DIRECTION

I would believe by this time that you are willing to hearken unto, and likewise follow, some directions as to how to become sincere converts. Directions on how to get ease when you are in pain, how to recover health when you are sick, or an estate which you have lost, I am confident would be heeded. And are not directions from the infallible Word of truth of far greater consequence?

The directions are these which follow:

1. Think upon, and with a serious spirit consider,

The Conversion of a Sinner

your ways. This consideration had great influence upon the Psalmist, Ps.119:59, *"I thought on my ways, and turned my feet unto Thy testimonies. I made haste and delayed not."* That injunction is doubled in Haggai 1:5, and again in verse 7, *"Thus saith the Lord of Hosts, Consider your ways."* And that passage in Ezek. 18:14 is to be observed, *"Now lo, if he beget a son that seeth all his father's sins which he hath done and considereth and doth not such like...."*

If sinners would but consider what they do when they do evil, it would be a means to make them cease to do evil and learn to do well. Consider the misery and danger of being at a distance from God. The ways you naturally walk in lead you away from Him, and the Scripture says, *"Those that are far from God shall perish, He will destroy all them that go a-whoring from Him,"* Ps.73:27. Think of these things so long until you find your hearts affected so as to conclude it the height of madness to lie secure in an unconverted state. Let this thought make a deep impression: all the while you persist in your evil ways you forsake the Lord and forsake your own mercies, and are travelling quickly to the regions of eternal woe and darkness!

2. Study the vanity of former excuses. I know the natural man's mouth is very full of them, but it is very easy to answer them.

"Sin," you say, "is riveted in my very nature."

Therefore you need to cry to heaven that your

The Conversion of a Sinner

nature may be changed.

"But sin is the common practice."

Therefore your danger is the greater and you should be more careful, lest you are overwhelmed in the ruin that will be so general.

"But my lusts are profitable and pleasant, and why should I abandon them?"

Consider, soul, whether the damned who have lost their souls and their eternal blessedness and suffer the vengeance of eternal fire have any reason to boast of gain or pleasure.

"But men will deride and scorn me if I become a convert."

They that do so are beside themselves, and sober people need not be concerned at the laughter of such as are out of their wits. Oh, condemn their contempt, despise the shame they cast upon you. Shortly they themselves will wish that, instead of scorning you, they had been imitators of you.

"But to turn to and follow God is very hard, and the difficulty is a very great discouragement."

The work is hard indeed, but the strength and assistance is great which shall be offered. The Lord will work all your works in you and for you, Is.26:12. He commands nothing but what He is ready to help you to perform Himself.

"But if I am a convert, I shall never live a pleasant hour. My tears shall be my meat and drink and my

The Conversion of a Sinner

sorrows shall be my perpetual companions."

Oh, gross mistake! Unreasonable prejudice against the ways of holiness! If godliness is so melancholy a business, why does the Scripture tell us of a peace which passes all understanding and joys that are unspeakable and full of glory? Why is David so often singing, so often harping, if mirth and religion were altogether inconsistent?

"Oh, but if I turn, I shall be exposed to suffering."

Well, suppose you are. The sufferings of this present time are not worthy to be compared with the present grace and consolation which will attend your trials, much less with the glory that shall be revealed.

Study the vanity of all such excuses!

3. Save yourselves from the stubborn generation you live among. This was the advice the Apostle gave to them that had been awakened and pricked in their hearts, Acts 2:40. You must shake hands with your former brethren in iniquity, else they will be a great temptation and snare to you. Carnal company is an incarnate devil who endeavors to draw as many as he can to hell along with him. Therefore, the wisest of men uses so many words of caution, Prov.4:14-15, *"Enter not into the path of the wicked, and go not in the way of evil men."* Avoid it, pass not by it, turn from it and pass away. Though you are not bound to be morose and uncivil towards the ungodly, take heed of being

The Conversion of a Sinner

delightfully familiar. Many a conviction and good resolution has cooled and vanished by our lighting into the society of the wicked. Suck not in any prejudices from them against true piety, and when they presume to prate against prayer, hearing, fasting, professing, when they quarrel against the Lord's Day and censure the Lord's people, look upon all this but as the ravings of such as are distracted, in a spiritual sense.

4. Despise not prophecyings. The ministry of the Word is ordained on purpose to work faith and to turn sinners unto God. Therefore, let not drowsiness, distraction, cares, pleasures, lusts, or the deceitfulness of riches choke this Word and hinder it from prospering to the end whereunto it is appointed. When Ezekiel prophesied over the dead and dry bones, they presently revived and a valley of dead bones became a living army. And who knows, while you are prophesied over by the ministry of the gospel, all of a sudden you may be made alive who were dead in trespasses. Let powerful preaching be prized and frequented by you. Certainly the Word has a converting power when it is set home, Ps.19:7, *"The Law of the Lord is perfect, converting the soul. The testimony of the Lord is sure, making wise the simple."*

5. Quench not the Spirit, I Thess. 5:19. You must not stifle His conviction but improve it. The Spirit of the Lord sometimes approaches very near unto a

The Conversion of a Sinner

drunkard, a swearer, a covetous worldling, an unclean person, and tells them the way they take is perverse before them, that there is but a step between them and death, between them and damnation. Therefore it moves them to humiliation and to reformation. He informs them that they had better leave their sins than be undone for their sake. Now such conviction might be heightened unto conversion if they were but closed with and improved, but thousands resist the Holy Ghost. They would rather be permitted to sin without disturbance than to have the waters troubled, though upon stepping in they might be healed, whatever their spiritual malady and plague is. Do you find the Spirit near you? Oh, heed His checks. Comply with all His motions and beg that you may not be put off with common operations, but that a saving work may be wrought in you!

6. Lay hold upon and plead the Lord's own covenant. In this covenant He has engaged to give you a new heart, to cleanse you from your filthiness and your idols, to put His Spirit within you and cause you to walk in His statutes, Ezek.36:25-27, that is, in one word, to convert you. Be earnest that these promises may be accomplished. Resolve that you will not take "no" for an answer. The Lord will be pleased with your importunity in a matter which is so much for His own honor to grant you. You cannot turn yourselves, but He can as easily do this work as leave it undone. One

The Conversion of a Sinner

word of life and power will raise you. And since He says, *"Turn ye, turn ye from your evil ways, for why will ye die, O house of Israel?"* then make this text into a prayer! "Turn us, turn us from our evil ways, for why should we die, O God of Israel?"

FINIS

The One Thing Necessary

Preached in a Sermon
at Paul's
Before the Right Honorable
Lord Mayor, and
the Aldermen of
the City of London.
(Aug.31, 1656)

by Thomas Watson
Pastor of St. Stephens, Walbrook
in the City of London

"How shall we escape, if we
neglect so great salvation?"
(Hebrews 2:3)

The One Thing Necessary

To the Right Honorable
John Dethick,
Lord Mayor of the City of London

Right Honorable,

It was not in my thoughts to have published this sermon (I looked upon it as too home-spun), but it was your Lordship's request to me at the first, and I have since received an invitation from your honorable court to that purpose. I knew not how to deny, lest while I did shun your loving commands I should fall under your just censure. My Lord, it was my design in this sermon to call you off from the empty, high-flown notions and litigious disputes of these times to look after that which is more solid, and wherein, I am sure, every man is very nearly concerned, viz. the working out of his salvation. It is a work that may call forth the most spiritual, vigorous actings of the soul in the prosecution of it. That work had need be well done which is for eternity.

My Lord, this is the true wisdom: to be wise to salvation, I Tim.5:15. By this godly policy we shall go beyond all the politicians of the times. We shall escape hell. We shall be raised to the true seat of honor. God will be our Father, Christ our Brother, the Spirit our Comforter, the angels our companions. When we die,

The One Thing Necessary

we shall carry a good conscience with us and leave a good name behind us. I shall not further expatiate. I desire that this sermon may come under your Honor's patrociny. Some little addition you will find in the end of it which I had before prepared for you but lacked time to serve it in. The Lord enoble you with His Spirit and crown you with soul-prosperity, which shall be the prayer of him who is,

From my study at
Stephens, Walbrook
October 15, 1656

Your Honors in all
Gospel Service,
Thomas Watson

Philippians 2:12

"...work out your own salvation with fear and trembling..."

If there is anything excellent, it is salvation. If there is anything necessary, it is working out salvation. If there is any tool to work with, it is holy fear: *"work out your salvation with fear."*

The words are a grave and serious exhortation, needful not only for those Christians who live in the time of the Apostles, but it may be fitly calculated for the meridian of this age wherein we live.

In the text observe first the manner of insinuation.

"My beloved" The Apostle labored by all means to ingratiate and wind himself into the hearts of the Philippians. He prescribes a gospel pill and dips it in sugar that it may go down better. He labors to possess the Philippians of this maxim, that whatever he spoke to them about their souls was purely in love. Sometimes he steeps his words in tears and speaks weeping, Phil.3:8. Sometimes he dips them in honey. Paul knew how to reprove. It was part of his office and a piece of his spiritual surgery. *"Rebuke them sharply,"* Titus 1:13, or as the Greek says, "cuttingly." But when he had finished lancing, he knew how to pour wine and oil

The One Thing Necessary

into the wound. He holds forth the breast as a nurse, and is willing to impart not only his sermon to the people, but his soul, I Thess.2:7-8.

And herein the Apostle Paul sets an example to all the ministers of Christ. Their hearts must be fired not with heat of passion but with love towards their people. They are Christ's ambassadors and must come with an olive branch of peace in their mouths. *"If I speak with the tongue of angels, and have not love, I am as sounding brass, and a tinkling cymbal,"* I Cor. 13:1. It is better to love as a pastor than to speak as an angel. Love is that flower of delight which should grow in the heart and send forth its perfume in the lips of every minister. Those who come in a spirit of meekness to their people are likely to do the most good. Knotty hearts will be soonest worked on by love. The fire will go where the wedge cannot. The thunderbolt may break, but the sun melts. When love sends forth its sweet influence, it melts a sinner's heart into tears. The joints being hard and stiff, rubbing them with oil makes them supple. The best way to soften a hard heart and make it tender is to ply it with this oil of love. And thus much for the manner of insinuation, *"My beloved."*

I proceed now to the exhortation itself, *"Work out your own salvation with fear and trembling,"* which words branch themselves into three particulars.

First, the act: *"work out."* Secondly, the object:

-169-

The One Thing Necessary

"your own salvation." Thirdly, the modus, or the manner how we should work it out, *"with fear and trembling."* I shall speak principally of the first two, and draw in the other briefly in the application.

The proposition is this, that it should be a Christian's great work to be working out his salvation. The great God has put us into the world as a vineyard, and here is the work He has set us about, the working out of salvation. There is a parallel Scripture to this in II Pet.1:10, *"give diligence to make your calling and election sure."* When estate, friends, or life cannot be made sure, let this be made sure. The Greek word signifies to study or to beat the brains about a thing. The word in the text, *"work out,"* implies two things. First, it implies a shaking off of spiritual sloth. Sloth is a pillow on which many have slept the sleep of death. And secondly, it implies a uniting and rallying together of all the powers of our souls that we may intend the business of salvation. God enacted a law in paradise that no man should eat of the tree of life but in the sweat of his brow.

That which is called "working" in the text has various appelations in Scripture. First, it is sometimes called "striving," Luke 13:29, *"strive to enter in at the strait gate."* Strive as if in agony or a bloody sweat. Secondly, it is sometimes called "seeking," Matt.6:33, *"Seek ye first the kingdom of God,"* as a man that has lost a treasure seeks diligently for it. We have lost

The One Thing Necessary

salvation. Adam, by eating of the tree of knowledge, lost the tree of life. Now seek, take David's candle and lantern and seek for salvation. The word "seek," as a learned writer notes, signifies to pursue a thing with enflamed desires, as a condemned man desires a pardon.

Thirdly, it is sometimes called "running in a race," I Cor.9:24, *"so run that ye may obtain."* The Apostle seems to allude to the games of Olympus which were celebrated every fifth year in honor of Jupiter. In those games they put forth all their strength. It is a long race from earth to heaven, so lay aside all the weights of sin which will hinder you in the race and reach forward with a winged swiftness to lay hold upon the mark.

Fourthly, it is sometimes called "offering violence to heaven," Matt.11:12, *"The kingdom of heaven suffers violence."* There must not only be diligence, but there must be violence. We must not only pray, but pray fervently, James 5:16. We must not only repent, but be zealous and repent, Rev.3:19; not only love, but be sick of love, Canticles 2:5. This is offering violence. The Greek word is a metaphor taken from a castle that holds out in a siege and will not be taken unless it is stormed. So the kingdom of heaven holds out against a supine, lazy Christian, and will not be taken but by storm.

I now proceed to the reasons enforcing this holy sweat and industry about salvation, and they are three.

The One Thing Necessary

We must work out out salvation because of:
* The difficulty of this work;
* The rareness of this work;
* The possibility of this work.

The difficulty of this work. It is a work that may make us labor to the going down of the sun of our life. Now this difficulty about the work of salvation will appear four manner of ways.

First, from the nature of the work. There is a metamorphosis to be worked. The heart must be changed, it is the very nursery of sin. It is the magazine where all the weapons of unrighteousness lie. It is a lesser hell. The heart is full of antipathy against God. It is angry with converting grace. Now that the bypass of the heart should be changed, what a work is this! How we should beg Christ that He who turned water into wine would use the water, or rather the poison, of nature into the wine of grace!

Secondly, the current of life is to be altered. That the tide of sin, which before ran so strong, should be turned is not easy. That the sinner, who before was falling hellward and wanted neither wind nor tide to carry him, should now alter his course and sail to a new port, this is a work indeed! It was by a miracle that the river Jordan was driven back, To see the earthly man become heavenly, to see a sinner move contrary to himself in the ways of Christ and holiness is as strange

The One Thing Necessary

as to see the earth fly upward or the bowl run contrary to its own bypass.

Salvation work is difficult in regard of the deceits about the work. The heart is ready to take many false stitches in this work of salvation. It has the heart of self-deceit, like those that can cog a die. Therefore Austin cries out, "The heart is a great deep." The heart is apt to be deceived about this work of salvation two ways.

1. It will often make a man take morality for grace. Alas, morality is but nature refined, old Adam put in a better dress. A moralized man is but a tame devil! There may be a fair stream of civility running and yet much vermin of pride and atheism lying at the bottom. The garnishment of moral excellencies is but setting a garland of flowers upon a dead man. How easy is it to be deceived in the business of salvation and, with Ixion, to embrace a cloud instead of Juno? Civility is not grace, though it is a good wall to plant the vine of grace against.

2. The heart will be ready to deceive us in this work of salvation and make us take a show of grace for grace. Pliny said that there is a beryl stone that resembles the true diamond. So there is something that looks like grace that is not. There are two graces which help much to the working out of salvation and we are soon deceived in them. First, repentance. True repentance is when we weep for sin as sin, when we weep for it because it is a defiling thing. It blots the image of God and stains the virginity of the soul. As it is an act of unkindness, it is a kicking against the breast that gives us milk. But how easy is it to prevaricate in this?

A. Many think they repent when it is not the offence but the penalty that troubles them; not the treason, but the bloody axe.

B. They think they repent when they shed a few tears, but though this ice begins to melt a little, it freezes again and they still go on in sin. Many weep for their unkind dealings with God, as Saul did for his unkindness to David. *"He said to David, Thou art more righteous than I for thou hast rewarded me good, whereas I have rewarded thee evil,"* I Sam.26. So men can lift up their voice and weep for sin, yet follow their sins again. They are like a snake that casts off its coat, but keeps its sting. There is as much difference between false and true tears as between channel water and spring water.

Second, another grace conducible to salvation is faith, but how easily are men deceived with a counterfeit pearl! There is this deceit about faith: when men apply the promises of the Word, but not the precepts. The promise is salvation, the precept is "working out." They will take the one but not the other, as if a physician should prescribe two receipts to his patient, a pill and a julip. He will take the julip because it is pleasant, but not the pill. Many will take Christ as a

The One Thing Necessary

Saviour, but refuse Him as a Prince; receive His benefits, but not submit to His laws. This is to put asunder what God has joined together. There being, therefore, such mistakes and deceits about this work of salvation, we need to be all the more cautious and curious in this work.

Thirdly, the difficulty about salvation work arises from the remoras and hindrances of this work. These hindrances are either (1) from within, viz. the flesh. This is a sly enemy. The flesh cries out for ease, *"it lusts against the Spirit,"* Gal.5:17. We are bid to crucify the flesh, Gal.5:24, but how many wounds must we give with the sword of the Spirit before the flesh will be perfectly crucified?

(2) We meet with hindrances in this work from without from temptations. Austin said our whole life is a temptation. We tread among snares. There is a snare in company recreation, yes, our table is often a snare. Satan is still fishing for our souls. How often does he lay a train of temptation to blow up our fort of grace? The Apostle tells us of his fiery darts, Eph.6:16. Temptations are called darts for their swiftness, they are shot in swiftly, and fiery for their terribleness. They are shot like flashes of fire into the soul which amaze and frighten, and does not this retard the work of salvation and make it difficult?

From reproaches. *"This sect is everywhere spoken against,"* Acts 28:22. The old serpent is ever spitting

The One Thing Necessary

his venom at religion and the professors of it. I may allude to that verse in I Cor.10:1, *"All our fathers were under a cloud."* All the saints of old have passed to heaven under a cloud of rude language and reproach. The world puts them in their black book whom God will put in His book in red letters! The throat of the wicked is an open sepulchre to bury the good names of those who have been the ensign-bearers of religion and have carried her colors.

Sometimes they have been defamed and slandered. Paul was reported to be a seditious man, II Tim.2:9. The Popish Rhemists defamed Calvin and blamed him for teaching that God was the author of sin and that he died cursing, though Beza, who was an eyewitness and wrote his life and death, confuted that slander and related what a comfortable end he had. Martin Bucer, that blessed man who cried out in a holy triumph, "I am Christ's and the devil has nothing to do with me," yet the Papists slanderously report that he denied that Christ was the Messiah come in the flesh. But he who was the orator at his funeral vouched for his character under oath. The Jesuites in Burgundia commit the same slander of Beza, that holy man. They say that he, perceiving death to be at hand, renounced his former profession of the gospel and was perfectly reconciled to the church at Rome. This was so false that Beza, who lived after the slander went abroad, himself refuted it with great indignation.

The One Thing Necessary

Sometimes the saints have had the trial of cruel mockings, Heb.11:36. Cyprian was called, in a jeer, Coprian; Athanasius, Satanus; David was the song of the drunkards, Ps.69:12. I do not doubt but that Noah had many a bitter taunt when he was building the ark so many years before the flood. They would laugh at him and censure him as an old, doting fool who would be wiser than all the world besides. Thus when we see the flood of God's wrath coming upon the world and we begin to build the ark and "work out salvation," men will be venting their scorn and derision: "What? You will be holier than others? More precise than necessary?" All this serves to retard salvation-work and make it difficult.

A third hindrance in this work is open violence, Gal.4:29, *"as he that was born after the flesh persecuted him that was born after the Spirit, so it is now."* No sooner does a man give up his name to Christ and seriously sets upon the working out of his salvation, but the world raises her trained bands and sets all the militia of hell against him. God's church is like Abraham's ram tied in a bush of thorns. Witness the ten persecutions in the time of Nero, Domitian, Trajan, etc. A man who is strictly holy is the target that is shot at. If the world's music will not prevail, it has its furnace ready, II Tim.3:12. Be assured that Christ and His cross are never parted. It is with us in our building for heaven as it was with the Jews in their building the

The One Thing Necessary

wall, *"everyone with one of his hands wrought the work, and with the other hand held a weapon,"* Neh.4:17. So we must not only be builders, but warriors. With one hand we must work, and with the other hand hold a weapon, viz. the sword of the Spirit, and fight the good fight of faith. This is yet another hindrance in the work. No sooner do we begin to set out for heaven, but *"bonds and afflictions abide us,"* Acts 20:23. The world sounds an alarm and there will be no cessation of arms until death.

That which makes salvation work hard is that it is a slippery work. Look *"to yourselves that we lose not those things which we have wrought,"* John 2:8. This work falls down almost as fast as we build. An ordinary craftsman, when he has been at work, finds his work the next morning just as he left it, but it is not so with us. When we have been working out salvation by prayer, fasting, and meditation, and we leave this work awhile, we shall not find our work as we left it. A great deal of our work will have fallen down again.

We need to be called upon often *"to strengthen the things which are ready to die,"* Rev.3:2. No sooner is a Christian taken off from the fire of the sanctuary, but he is ready to cool and freeze again in security. He is like a watch: when he has been wound up towards heaven, he quickly unwinds to earth and sin again. When the gold has been purified in the furnace, it remains pure, but it is not so with the heart. Let it be heated in an ordinance, let it be purged in the fire of affliction. It does not remain pure but quickly gathers oil and corruption. We are seldom long in a good frame. All this shows how difficult the work of salvation is. We must not only work, but set a watch, too!

QUESTION 1. But why has God made the way to heaven so hard? Why must there be this working?

ANSWER 1. To make us set a high estimate upon heavenly things. If salvation were easily come by, we should not have valued its worth. If diamonds were ordinary they would be slighted, but, because they are hard to come by, they are in great esteem. Tertullian said that when pearls grew common in Rome, people wore them on their shoes, which was the next way to tread them under their feet. Salvation is such a pearl as God will not have slighted. Therefore, it must be acquired by holy industry. God will not allow the price of spiritual mercies to fall. Those who would have this precious flower of salvation must gather it in the sweat of their brows.

We must work and take pains that we may be fitted for heaven. A father will give his son the inheritance, but first he will give him an education that he may be fit for it. God will settle salvation upon us, but first He *"makes us meet for the inheritance,"* Col.1:12. While we are working, we are running and fitting for heaven. Sin is weakening, grace is ripening. While we

The One Thing Necessary

are in combat, we are fitting for the crown. First you season the vessel before you pour in the wine. God will season us with grace before He pours in the wine of glory.

QUESTION 2. But if there must be this working, how is it said that Christ's yoke is easy?

ANSWER 2. To the fleshly part, it is hard, but where there is a new and holy principle infused, Christ's yoke is easy. It is not a yoke, but a crown. When the wheels of the soul are oiled with grace, then a Christian moves in the way of religion with facility and alacrity. A child delights in obeying his father. It was Paul's heaven to serve God, *"I delight in the law of God in the inner man,"* Rom.7:22. And how swiftly is the soul carried upon those wings! Christ's service is Christ's freedom, therefore the Apostle calls it *"a law of liberty,"* James 1:25.

To serve God, to love God, to enjoy God, is the sweetest liberty in the world. Christ does not, as did Pharaoh, *"make his people serve with rigor,"* Ex.1:13, but He lays upon them the *"constraints of love,"* II Cor.5:14. His precepts are not burdens, but privileges; not fetters, but ornaments. Thus His yoke is easy, but, to an unregenerate man, the yoke has a nail in it. It galls and vexes. As far as corruption prevails, the best heart finds some reluctancy. And so much for the first reason, the difficulty of the work.

The second reason why we must put forth so much

The One Thing Necessary

holy sweat and industry about salvation is because of the rareness of this work. Few shall be saved, therefore we need to work all the harder that we may be in the number of those few. The way to hell is a broad way, it is paved with riches and pleasure. It has a golden pavement, therefore there are so many travellers on it, but the way to heaven lies out of the road. It is an un-beaten path, and few can find it.

The criers of universal grace say that Christ died intentionally for all, but then why are not all saved? Can Christ be frustrated of His intention? Some are so gross as to aver that all shall actually be saved, but has our Lord Christ not told us, *"the gate is strait, and few there be that find it,"* Matt.7:14? How all can go in at this gate and yet but a few find it seems to me to be a paradox. The drove of men goes to shambles, *"but a remnant shall be saved,"* Rom.9:27. The whole piece is cut off and goes to the devil. Only a remnant shall be saved. Most of the people in the world are wind-falls. That olive tree in Is.17:16 with two or three olive berries on the top of the uppermost bough may be a fit emblem of the scarcity of those that shall be saved. Satan goes away with the harvest, God has only a few gleanings. In this great city, if it should go by vote and by poll, the devil would carry it.

Some of the learned observe that if you were to divide the world into thirty equal parts, nineteen of those thirty are overrun with heathenish idolatry, six

of the remaining eleven with the doctrine of Moham-
med, so that there remains but five parts of the thirty
where there is anything of Christianity. Among those
"Christians" are so many seduced Papists on the one
hand and formal Protestants on the other that surely
there are few that are saved. It being thus, it should
make us strive all the more that we may be of the number of those few who shall inherit salvation.

The third reason why we should put forth so much
vigor about the work of salvation is because of the
possibility of the work. Impossibility kills all endeavor. Who will take pains for that which he thinks
there is no hope of ever obtaining? But *"there is hope
in Israel concerning this,"* Ezra 10:2. Salvation is a
thing that is feasible, it may be had. O Christians,
though the gate of paradise is straight yet the gate is
open. It is shut against the devils but is open to you.
Who would not crowd hard to get in? It is put paring
off your sins, it is but unloading some of your thick
clay, it is but abating the swelling humor of your pride,
and you may get in at the straight gate. This possibility,
nay probability, of salvation may put your life into
your endeavor. If there is corn to be had, why should
you sit starving in your sins any longer?

USE 1. Information. It shows that salvation is not
as facile a thing as most imagine. Many fancy a fine,
easy way to heaven; a sigh, or tear, or "Lord, have

The One Thing Necessary

mercy," will save them. Those who believe this are in a golden dream. The text tells us of working out salvation. Basil compares the way to heaven to a man going over a narrow bridge. If he treads ever so much aside, he falls in and drowns. He that thinks the way is easy is never yet in the way. There are so many precepts to obey, so many promises to believe, so many temptations to resist that we shall not find the easy way.

There must not only be diligence, but violence. Beloved, heaven's gate is not like that iron gate which opened to Peter of its own accord, Acts 12:10. No, there must be knocking and striving. Jacob obtained the blessing in the garments of Esau. The name Esau in Hebrew signifies working. If you would wear this embroidered garment of salvation, you must have it by way of working, *"work out your own salvation."* Hannibal forged a way for his army over the Alps. We must forge our way to glory through difficulties. I like the example one man gave of a hand with a pick axe digging a way through a rock with this motto: "I WILL EITHER FIND A WAY OR MAKE ONE!"

We must go to heaven through sweat and blood. There is nothing gotten without hard labor. You cannot have the world without labor, and would you have Christ and salvation without it? Do men dig for lead and not much more for gold? It is observable that Adam in Paradise was not idle, but he dressed the vineyard. The angels themselves, though they are glorious spirits, are yet ministering spirits, Heb.1:14. God has put this diligence into creatures void of reason. The bee is a most industrious creature, all of them have their own work to do in the hive. Some of the bees trim the honey, some work the wax, some frame the comb, and others lie as sentinels at the door of the hive to keep out the drone. Is the bee so industrious by the instinct of nature in the working of honey? Oh, how industrious ought we to be in the working out of salvation!

USE 2. Reproof. Out of this text, as a spiritual quiver, I may draw several arrows of reproof.

1. It reproves those who prefer other things before salvation, who labor more for the bread that perishes than for salvation. Their chief care is how to live in the world and get a present subsistence. *"All the labor of a man is for his mouth,"* Ecc.6:7. The body shall be tended to and looked after, which is but the brutish part, but the poor soul is kept to hard commons. This is for Christians to turn into heathens, Matt.6, *"for after these things the Gentiles seek."* God never sent us here only to wear fine clothes or fare sumptuously every day, but that we should drive a trade for salvation. If this is not done, we have shot beside the mark all this while. We have but trimmed the scabbard and let the soul, that blade of admirable mettle, rust and canker.

The One Thing Necessary

2. It reproves such as, instead of working, stand idle all the day in the vineyard. They wish for salvation but do not work. The idle Christian is like a soldier that has a good mind to the spoil and treasure of a castle but is loath to put himself to any trouble or hazard. Men could be content to have salvation if it would, like the ripe figs of Nahum 3:12, *"fall into the mouth of the eater."* The sluggard *"puts his hand into his bosom,"* Prov.19:24, and is loath to pluck it out, though it is to lay hold of a crown. *"They stretch themselves upon the beds of ivory,"* Amos 6:4. Men would rather lie upon a soft bed than go to heaven in a fiery chariot of zeal.

Chrysostom calls idleness the root of despair. An idle Christian ravels out his time unprofitably. He stands in the world for a cipher, and be assured that God writes down no ciphers in the book of life. An idle person is a fit subject for the devil to work upon. We do not sow seed in fallow ground, but the devil sows most of his seed of temptation in hearts that lie fallow. Jerome makes this observation about the crabfish. While the oyster opens itself, the crabfish flings a little stone into its mouth so that the oyster cannot shut itself and so the crab devours it. The devil is like this crab when he takes men gaping (as is usual for those who are idle), then he throws in his stones of temptation and so devours them.

3. It reproves those who, instead of making religion a work, make it a play. These are they who have

The One Thing Necessary

found a new way to heaven, who make the way easier than ever did Christ! Such as tell us that there is no Law to a believer, and if there is no Law, then there is no transgression, and if there is no transgression, then no repentance is needed. Between the Arminian and the Antinomian, it is a very short cut to heaven. The Arminian says we have power in ourselves to believe, and the Antinomian says that a believer is not under any Law, he is bound to no duty. Christ has done all for him, so that by taking this stride he is presently in heaven. If this doctrine is true, then every day is a play-day, and the Apostle made a mistake when he said, *"work out your salvation."*

4. It reproves those that, instead of working out their salvation, dispute away their salvation; such as would dispute against the authority of Scripture and would make our faith a fable; such as dispute against the immortality of the soul and so at once would pull down the court of conscience; such as dispute against the divinity of Christ. This may be called, indeed, the doctrine of devils, I Tim.4:1. It is a doctrine diametrically opposed to that Scripture in I John 5:20, *"We are in Him that is true, even in His Son, Jesus Christ; this is the true God."* This text is a bulwark against the Socinian.

Oh, the patience of God, that those who open their mouths blasphemously against Christ, the earth does not open her mouth and swallow them up! That such should have any connivance who dare impugn the divinity of the Son of God is a lamentation, and shall be for a lamentation. Some of the best heathen writers (Livy, Aristotle, Plutarch) affirm that there were edicts and punishments enacted by heathen princes and states in matters of religion. A heathen would not suffer his god to be blasphemed, and shall Christians suffer it?

5. It reproves those who, instead of pursuing their own salvation, pursue their own destruction. These are profane persons who go to hell in the sweat of their own brows.

- Drunkards. What they get in the temple, they lose in the tavern. They steep the sermons they hear in wine. *"Woe to the drunkards in Ephraim,"* Is.28:1. I may change the word and say "the drunkards of England." There is a kind of wine you call lachryme, which signifies tears. Such a wine the damned drink of which is burned with the wrath of God, and this shall be the drunkard's cup.

- Swearers. They swear away their salvation. The swearer, it seems, has bad credit. He must stake down an oath or none will trust him. But let him remember he runs his soul into a warning, *"Swear not at all,"* Matt.5:34. If we must give an account for idle words, shall not idle oaths be put in the account book? When the scab breaks forth in the lip, that man is to be pronounced unclean. Every oath is a wound given to

The One Thing Necessary

soul, and every wound has a mouth to cry to heaven for vengeance. Some are boiled up to that height of wickedness that, like mad dogs, they fly in the face of heaven by cursing. And let a minister tell them of their sin, let him but go about to bring them home again, as the Law provided that one should bring home his neighbor's ass when he went astray, Ex.23:4, and they will kick against the reproof. Like lime, by pouring on the water of a reprehension, they are the more enflamed. These are upon the spur to damnation, but I will not touch this pitch any longer.

- Adulterers. The adulterer's heart, like the swearer's tongue, is set on fire by hell. Creatures void of reason will rise up in judgment against such. It is reported of the stork, that chaste creature, that it confines itself to its own nest, and if any of the storks leaves his own mate and joins with any other, the rest fall upon him and pluck his feathers from him. God would have the adulterer put to death, Deut.22:22. Gregory observes, concerning the stream of fire and brimstone poured upon Sodom, that God sent that noisesome plague to let them see the filthiness of their sin. This sin of adultery is a soul-damning sin, I Cor.6:9. The adulterer, like the fly, flies so long around the candle that at last he singes his soul. This sin, though it began comically, it ends tragically! Will it not be *"bitterness in the end,"* II Sam.2:26? This sweet calm is before an earthquake. After the woman's hair comes the lion's teeth.

6. It reproves those who are put off this great work of salvation until they are past their labor. They put off repenting until old age and sickness.

A. Until old age. When they are fit for no other work, then they will begin this. Old age is no good age to repent in. When the fingers are stiff, it is hard learning to play the lute. When the heart is grown hard and stiff in wickedness, it is hard to tune the penitential string. A tender plant is easily removed, but it is hard to pluck up an old tree that is rooted. An old sinner that has been a long time rooting in sin is hardly plucked out of his natural estate. In matters of salvation, it is dangerous to adjourn. The longer men go on in sin, the more full possession Satan has of them. The longer poison stays in the stomach, the more deadly.

It is madness to put off the work of salvation until evening and sunset. *"The night cometh when no man can work,"* John 9:4. It would be a very unwise course for a mariner, while the ship is sound, the tackling strong, the wind favorable, and the sea calm, to lie idle at anchor, and when the ship begins to leak and the tempest to rise, then to launch forth and hoist up sails for a voyage. So is he who neglects the time of health and strength, and when old age comes and his tackling is even broken, then begins his voyage toward heaven.

It is very questionable whether God will accept

repentance when it is so late. He calls for the first-fruits, and do we think to put Him off with the gleanings? This was not the least reason why God rejected Cain's offering, because it was so long before he brought it. *"In process of time, Cain brought the fruit of the ground,"* Gen.4:3, or, as the original is more emphatic, "at the end of many days." It seems it was stale before he brought it. How unworthy is this, for men to give the devil their strength and marrow and then to come and lay their old bones before God's altar? It is true God may show mercy at last, but such run a desperate hazard. A sinner, in the time of his old age, sleeps between death and the devil as Peter slept between two soldiers.

B. Until sickness. He would be very unwise who, preparing to go on a long journey, should lay the heaviest load on the weakest horse. What imprudence is it to lay the heavy load of repentance on yourself when you have been made feeble by sickness? When the hands shake, the lips quiver, the sinews shrink, the heart faints? Perhaps you shall have no time of sickness, perhaps you will not have the use of your senses. Perhaps God will deny you His grace and then where is your repentance? It is just that he who forgets God in the time of health, God should forget him in the time of sickness.

7. It reproves those who begin to work, but do not work out their salvation. It is not enough to begin well.

The One Thing Necessary

Some have, like Jehu, driven furiously in religion, but within awhile their chariot wheels have fallen off. We live in the fall of the leaf. We have observed several who once put forth fair blossoms and give good hopes of conversion, but their Spring is turned into Autumn. They have stopped working for heaven, a sign that the motion was only artificial, not vital. *"Israel hath cast off the thing that is good,"* Hos.8:3. Such as were once diligent and zealous in prayer, hearing, holy conference, now they have left off the thing that is good. They have tired in their march to heaven.

I have often thought that there are many who may be compared to Nebuchadnezzar's image in Daniel 3. At first they seemed to have a head of gold. They looked like glorious professors. Then afterwards they seemed to be silver, then brass, then iron, then clay. They have at last degenerated into sin. Thus, like fair mornings, they have soon become overcast. Epiphanius tells of the Gnostics that at first they seemed to be a strict, holy people, but afterwards fell to libertinism. Some have grown so impudent that they brag of their apostasy. Time was when they read and prayed in their families, but now they thank God that they have grown wiser and they cease from these duties. Just as if you should hear the devil boast that once he was an angel of light, but now he is turned into an angel of darkness. Apostates are the richest spoils that Satan goes away with. He will hang these up in hell for

The One Thing Necessary

triumph. Such as have left off working, let them read that thundering Scripture in II Pet.2:21, *"For it had been better for them not to have known the way of righteousness, than after they have known it to turn from the holy commandment."* By leaving off working, they unravel all that they have done before. They lose their reward. He that runs half the race and then faints loses the garland.

USE 3. And so I proceed to the next use which is of exhortation, to persuade you all in the bowels of Christ to set upon this great work, the working out of your salvation. Beloved, here is a plot for heaven, and I would have you all in this plot. Rally together all the powers of your souls. Give neither God nor yourselves rest until you have made your election sure. Christians, fall to work. Do it early, earnestly, incessantly. Pursue salvation as in a holy chase. Other things are but matters of convenience, salvation is a matter of necessity. Either you must do the work that Christians are doing or you must do the work that devils are doing. Oh, you that never yet took one stitch in this work of salvation, begin now. Religion is a good trade if it is well followed. Be assured that there is no salvation without working, but here I must lay down a caution to prevent mistakes.

CAUTION. Though we are not saved without working, yet we are not saved for our working. Bellarmine said we merit heaven out of unworthiness.

The One Thing Necessary

No, though we are saved in the use of means, yet by grace, too, Eph.2:5. There must be plowing and sowing the ground, but no crops can be expected without the influence of the sun. So there must be working, but no crop of salvation can be hoped for without the sunshine of free grace. *"Tis your Father's good pleasure to give you the kingdom,"* Luke 12:32. Give? "Why," some might say, "we have worked hard for it!" Aye, but heaven is a donation. Though you work for it, yet it is the good pleasure of God to bestow it. Still look up to Christ's merit. It is not your sweat but His blood that saves.

It is clear that your working cannot merit salvation, Phil.4:13, *"tis God that works in you to will, and to do."* It is not your working but God's co-working. For as the scrivener guides the child's hand or he cannot write, so the Spirit of God must afford His auxiliary concurrence or our work stands still. How, then, can any man merit by working when it is God that helps him to work? I should now, having laid down this caution, re-assume the exhortation and persuade you to the working out of salvation, but I must first remove two objections which lie in the way.

OBJECTION 1. You bid us to work out salvation, but we have no power to work.

ANSWER 1. It is true, we have no power. I deny that we have free will. Man, before conversion, is purely passive. Therefore the Scripture calls it, *"a* *heart of stone,"* Ezek.36. A man in his pure, natural state can no more prepare himself to his own converting than the stone can prepare itself to its own softening. But yet, when God begins to draw, we may follow. Those dry bones in Ezekiel could not, of themselves, live, but when breath came into them, then *"they lived and stood upon their feet,"* Ezek.37:10.

QUESTION. But suppose God has not dropped in a principle of grace? Suppose He has not caused breath to enter?

ANSWER. Yet use the means. Though you cannot work spiritually, yet work physically. Do what you are able to do, and that for two reasons.

1. Because a man, by neglecting the means, destroys himself, as a man, by not sending for the physician, may be said to be the cause of his own death.

2. God is not wanting to us when we do what we are able. Urge the promise, *"seek and ye shall find,"* Matt.7:7. Put this bond in suit by prayer. You say you have no power, but have you not a promise? Act as far as you can. Though I dare not say, as the Arminian, when we exert and put forth nature God is bound to give grace, yet I do say God is not wanting to them that seek His grace. Nay, I will say more. He denies His grace to none but them that willfully refuse it.

OBJECTION 2. The second objection is this: But to what purpose should I work? There is a decree passed. If God has decreed I shall be saved, I shall be saved.

ANSWER 2. God decrees salvation in a way of working, II Thess.2:13. Origen, in his book against Celsus, observes a subtle argument of some who disputed about fate and destiny. One gave counsel to his sick friend not to send for the physician because, he said, it is appointed by destiny whether you shall recover or not. If it is your destiny to recover, then you do not need the physician, and if it is not your destiny, then the physician will do you no good.

The same fallacy is used by the devil against men. He bids them not to work. If God has decreed that they shall be saved, they shall be saved and there is no need of working. If He has not decreed their salvation, then their working will do them no good. This is an argument fetched out of the devil's reasoning. But we say that God decrees the end in the use of the means. God decreed that Israel should enter into Canaan, but first they must fight with the sons of Anak. God decreed that Hezekiah should recover out of his sickness, but let him lay a fig to the boil, Is.38:21.

We do not argue this way in other things. A man does not say, " If God has decreed that I shall have a crop this year, I shall have a crop! What need do I have to plow, or sow, or fertilize the land?" No, he will use the means and expect a crop. Though *"the blessing of the Lord makes rich,"* Prov. 10:23, yet it is as true, *"the diligent hand makes rich,"* Prov. 10:4. God's

The One Thing Necessary

decreeing is carried on by our working.

And thus, having removed these objections out of the way, let me now persuade you to set upon this blessed work, the working out of your salvation. And, that my words might better prevail, I shall propound several arguments by way of motive to excite you to this work.

1. The first argument or motive to working is taken from the preciousness of the soul. Well may we take pains that we may secure this from danger. The soul is a divine spark kindled by the breath of God. It out-balances the world, Matt.16:26. If the world is the book of God, as Origen calls it, the soul is the image of God. Plato calls the soul a glass of the Trinity. It is a bright mirror in which some refracted beams of God's wisdom and holiness shine forth. The soul is a blossom of eternity.

God has made the soul capable of communion with Himself. It would bankrupt the world to give half the price of a soul. How highly did Christ value the soul when He sold Himself to buy it? Oh, then, what a pity is it that this excellent soul, this soul for which God called a council in heaven when He made it, should miscarry and be undone to all eternity? Who would not rather work night and day than lose such a soul? The jewel is invaluable, the loss irreparable.

2. Holy activity and industry enobles a Christian.

The One Thing Necessary

The more excellent anything is, the more active it is. The sun is a glorious creature. It never stands still but is always going on its circuit around the world. Fire is the purest element and the most active, it is ever sparkling and flaming. The angels are the most noble creatures and the most nimble. Therefore, they are represented by cherubim with their wings displayed. God Himself is a most pure act.

Homer said of Agamemnon that he sometimes resembled Jupiter in feature, Pallas in wisdom, Mars in valor. By holy activity we resemble God who is a most pure act. The phoenix flies with a coronet on its head. The industrious Christian does not need a coronet, his sweat enobles him. His labor is his ensign of honor. Solomon tells us that *"drowsiness clothes a man with rags,"* Prov.23:21. Infamy is one of the rags that hang upon him. God hates a dull temper. We read in the Law that the ass, being a dull creature, must not be offered up in sacrifice. Spiritual activity is a badge of honor.

3. Working out salvation is that which will make heaven and death sweet to us.

A. It will sweeten death. He that has been hard at work all day, how quietly does he sleep at night? You that have been working out your salvation all your lives, how comfortably may you lay down your head at night in the grave upon a pillow of dust in hope of a glorious resurrection? This will be a deathbed cordial.

The One Thing Necessary

B. It will sweeten heaven. The more pains we have taken for heaven, the sweeter it will be when we come there. It is delightful for a man to look over his work and see the fruit appear. When he has been planting trees in his orchard or setting flowerings, it is pleasant to behold and review his labors. Thus in heaven, when we shall see the fruit of our labors, *"the end of our salvation,"* I Pet.1:9, this will make heaven the sweeter. The more pains we have taken for heaven, the more welcome it will be. The more sweat, the more sweet. When a man has been sinning, the pleasure is gone and the sting remains, but when he has been repenting, the labor is gone and the joy remains.

4. You still have time to work. This text and sermon would be out of season to preach to the damned in hell. If I should bid them work, it is too late. Their time is past. It is night with the devil, it is still day with you. *"Work while it is day,"* John 9:4. If you lose your day, you lose your souls. This is the season for your souls. Now God commands, now the Spirit breathes, now ministers beseech, and as so many bells of Aaron would chime in your souls to Christ, oh, improve the season. This is your seed time, now sow the seeds of faith and repentance. If when you have seasons you lack hearts, the time may come when you have hearts and shall lack seasons. Take time while you may. The mariner hoists up his sails while the wind blows. Never did a people have a fairer gale for heaven than

The One Thing Necessary

you of this city do, and will you not set forward in your voyage? What riding is there to the term? I assure you the Lawyer will not lose His term. Oh, my brethren, now is the term-time for your souls. Now plead with God for mercy, or at least get Christ to plead for you.

Think seriously on these eight things.

First, our life unravels swiftly. Gregory compares our life to the mariner in a ship going full sail. We are every day sailing swiftly to eternity.

Secondly, the seasons of grace, though they are precious, yet they are not permanent. Abused mercies will, like Noah's dove, take their wings and fly from us. England's golden hour will soon run out. Gospel blessings are very sweet but very swift. *"Now they are hid from thine eyes,"* Luke 19:42. We know not how soon the golden candlesticks may be removed.

Thirdly, there is a time when the Spirit has finished striving. There are certain tides of the Spirit, and, these being neglected, it is possible that we may never see another tide come in. When conscience has finished speaking, usually the Spirit has stopped striving.

Fourthly, the loss of gospel opportunities will be the hell of hell. When a sinner shall think with himself at the last day, "Oh, what I might have been! I might have been as rich as the angels, as rich as heaven could make me. I had a season to work in , but I lost it." This will be as a vulture gnawing upon him. This will enhance and accent his misery, and let all this persuade

The One Thing Necessary

you speedily to work out your salvation.

Fifthly, you may do this work and not hinder your other work. Working out salvation and working in a calling are not inconsistent. And this I insert to prevent an objection. Some may say, "But I work so hard for heaven that I shall have no time for my trade." Be sure that the wise God would never make any of His commands to interfere. As He would have you seek His kingdom, Matt.6:33, so He would have you provide for your family, I Tim.5:8. You may drive two trades together. I do not like those who make the church exclude the shop, who swallow up all their time in hearing but neglect their work at home, II Thess. 3:11. They are like the lilies of the field, *"which toil not, neither do they spin,"* Matt.6:28. God never sealed any warrant to idleness. He both commands and commends diligence in a calling, which may rather encourage us to look after salvation, because this work will not take us off our other work. A man may follow God fully with Caleb, Num.14:34, and yet with David, *"follow the ewes great with young,"* Ps.78:71. Piety and industry may dwell together.

Sixthly, the inexcusableness of those that neglect working out their salvation. I think I hear God expostulating the case with men at the last day after this manner, "Why did you not work? I gave you time to work, I gave you light to work by, I gave you My gospel, My Spirit, My ministers. I bestowed talents on

The One Thing Necessary

you to trade, I set the recompence of reward before you. Why did you not work out your salvation? Either it must be sloth or stubbornness. Was there any work you did of greater concern? You could work in brick, but not in gold. What can you say for yourselves as to why the sentence should not be passed." Oh, how will the sinner be left speechless at such a time, and how will this cut him to the heart to think how he neglected salvation and could give no reason for it.

Seventhly, the inexpressible misery of those who do not work out salvation. Those that sleep in spring shall beg in harvest. After death, when they look to receive a full crop of glory, they will be put to beg for one drop of water as did Dives. Vagrant persons who will not work are sent to the house of corrections. Such as will not work out salvation, let them know that hell is God's house of correction that they must be sent to.

If all this does not prevail, consider lastly what it is we are working for. None will take pains for a trifle. We are working for a crown, for a throne, for a paradise, and all this is comprised in that one word "salvation." Here is a whet-stone to industry. All men desire salvation. It is the crown of our hopes. We should not think any labor too much for this. What pains will men take for earthly crowns and scepters! And suppose the kingdoms of the world were more illustrious than they are, their foundations of gold, their walls of pearl, their windows of sapphire. What

The One Thing Necessary

is all this to that kingdom we are laboring for? We may as well span the firmament as set forth this in all its splendor and magnificence.

Salvation is a beautiful thing. It is as far above our thoughts as it is above our deserts. Oh, how should this add wings to our endeavors! The merchant will run through the intemperate zones of heat and cold for a little prize. The soldier, for a rich booty, will endure the bullet and the sword. He will gladly undergo a bloody spring for a golden harvest. Oh, then, how much more should we spend our holy sweat for this blessed prize of salvation!

And so, having laid down some arguments by way of motive to persuade us to this work, I shall now propound some means by way of direction to help us in this work. And here I shall show you what are those things to be removed which will hinder our working, and what are those things to be followed which will further it.

We must remove those things which will hinder our working out salvation. There are six bars in the way to salvation which must be removed.

1. The entanglements of the world. While the foot is in a snare, a man cannot run. The world is a snare. While our feet are in it, we cannot *"run the race that is set before us,"* Heb.12:1. If a man were to climb up a steep rock with weights tied to his legs, they would hinder his ascent. Too many golden weights will

The One Thing Necessary

hinder us from climbing up this steep rock that leads to salvation. While the mill of a trade is going, it makes such a noise that we can hardly hear the minister lifting up his voice like a trumpet. The world chokes our zeal and appetite for heavenly things. The earth puts out our fire, the music of the world charms us to sleep and then we cannot work. In gold mines there are deadly gasses. Oh, how many souls have been destroyed with a gas arising from the earth!

2. The second bar in the way to salvation is sadness and uncheerfulness. When a man's heart is sad, he is unfit to go about his work, he is like an untuned instrument. Under fears and discouragements we act but faintly in religion. David labors to chide himself out of this spiritual melancholy, *"Why art thou cast down, O my soul?"* Ps.42:5. Cheerfulness quickens. The Lacedemonians used music in their battles to excite their spirits and make them fight more valiantly. Cheerfulness is like music to the soul, it excites to duty. It oils the wheels of the affections. Cheerfulness makes service come off with delight, and we are never carried so swift in religion as upon the wings of delight. Melancholy takes off our chariot wheels and then we drive on heavily.

3. The third bar to salvation is spiritual sloth. This is a great impediment to our working. It was said of Israel, *"they despised the pleasant land,"* Ps.106:24. What should be the reason? Canaan was a paradise of

The One Thing Necessary

delight, a type of heaven. Aye, but they thought it would cost them a great deal of trouble and hazard to get it, and they would rather go without it. They despised the pleasant land. Are there not millions among us who would rather go sleeping to hell than sweating to heaven? I have read of certain Spaniards who live near where there is a great store of fish, yet they are so lazy that they will not take the pains to catch them. They buy them off of their neighbors! Such a sinful stupidity and sloth is upon most so that, though Christ is near them, though salvation is offered in the gospel, yet they will not work out salvation. *"Slothfulness casts into a deep sleep,"* Prov.19:15. Adam lost his rib when he was asleep, and many a man loses his soul in this deep sleep.

4. The fourth bar in the way to salvation is an opinion of the easiness of salvation: "God is merciful, and if worst comes to worst, we need only to repent."

God is merciful, it is true, but with all He is just. He must not wrong His justice by showing mercy. Therefore, observe that clause in the proclamation, Ex.34:6, *"He will by no means clear the guilty."* If a king proclaimed that only those should be pardoned who came in and submitted to his scepter, could any still persisting in rebellion claim the benefit of that pardon? Oh, sinner, would you have mercy, and will you not disband the weapons of unrighteousness?

"Only repent?" It is such an "only" that we cannot

The One Thing Necessary

hit unless God directs our arrow. Tell me, oh sinner, is it easy for a dead man to live and walk? You are spiritually dead and wrapped up in your winding sheet, Eph.2:2. Is regeneration easy? Are there no pangs in the new birth? Is self-denial easy? Do you know what religion must cost, and what it may cost? It must cost you parting with your lusts, and it may cost you parting with your life! Take heed of this obstruction. Salvation is not *per saltum*. It is not a walk through the forest. Thousands have gone to hell upon this mistake. The broad spectacles of presumption have made the straight gate seem wider than it is.

5. The fifth bar in the way to salvation is carnal friends. It is dangerous to listen to their voice. The serpent spoke in Eve. Job's wife would have called him off from serving God, *"dost thou still retain thine integrity?"* Job 2:9. What, still pray and weep? Here the devil handed a temptation to Job through his wife. Carnal friends will be calling us off from our work. "What is the need for all this ado? Less pains will serve."

We read that some of Christ's kindred, when they saw Christ so earnest in His preaching, would have checked Him, Mark 3:21, *"His friends went to lay hold on Him."* Our friends and kindred would sometimes stand in our way to heaven, and, judging our zeal as madness, would lay hold of us and hinder us from working out our salvation. Such friends Spira

-205-

The One Thing Necessary

met with, seeking their advice as to whether he should revoke his former opinion concerning Luther's doctrine or persist in it to his death. They wished him to recant, and so, openly adjuring his former faith, he became like a living man in hell.

6. The sixth bar in the way to salvation is evil company. They will take us off our work. Sweet waters lose their freshness when they run into salt water. Christians lose their freshness and savor among the wicked. Christ's doves will be sullied by *"lying among these pots,"* Ps.68:13. Sinful company is like the water in a blacksmith's forge which quenches the iron, be it never so hot. Such people cool good affections. The wicked have the *"plague of the heart,"* I Kings 8:38, and their breath is infectious. They will discourage us from working out our salvation.

If a man were a suitor to a woman and very earnest in his pursuit of her, and then one came to him with a bad report of her, some impediment, he would, upon hearing this, cease his pursuit of her. So it is with many a man who begins to be a suitor of religion. He would willingly have the match made up, and he grows very hot and violent in the suit and sets to working out his salvation, but then somes of his confederates come and tell him that they know something bad about religion. *"This sect is everywhere spoken against,"* Acts 28:21. There must be so much strictiness and mortification that he must never look to see a good day

The One Thing Necessary

again. Hereupon he is discouraged and so the match is broken off. Take heed of such persons, they are devils covered with flesh. They are, as one has said, like Herod, who would have killed Christ as soon as He was born. Thus, when Christ is beginning to be formed in the heart, they would, in a spiritual sense, kill Him.

And thus I have shown you the bars that lie in the way to salvation which must be removed.

I now proceed, in the second place, to lay down some helps conducive to salvation.

The first is in the text, *"fear and trembling."* This is not a fear of doubting, but a fear of diligence. This fear is requisite in the working out of salvation. *"Let us fear lest we come short,"* Heb.4:1. Fear is a remedy against presumption. Fear is that flaming sword that turns every way to keep sin from entering. Fear quickens, it is an antidote against sloth. *"Noah, being moved with fear, prepared an ark,"* Heb.11:8. The traveller, fearing lest night should overtake him before he gets to his journey's end, spurs on the faster.

Fear causes circumspection. He that walks in fear treads warily. Fear is a preservative against apostasy, *"I will put My fear in your hearts, and you shall not depart from Me,"* Jer.32:40. The fear of falling keeps us from falling. Fear is the badge and livery of a Christian. The saints of old were men fearing God, Mal.3:17. It is reported of holy Anselm that he spent most of his thoughts about the day of judgment. *"Blessed is he*

The One Thing Necessary

that fears always," Prov.28:14. Fear is a Christian's garrison, the way to be secure is always to fear. This is one of the best tools for a Christian to work with.

Secondly, another great help in working out salvation is love. Love makes the work come off with delight. Seven year's labor seemed as nothing to Jacob because of the love that he bore for Rachel. Love facilitates everything. It is like wings to the bird, like wheels to the chariot, like sails to the ship. It carries on swiftly and cheerfully in duty. Love is never weary. It is an excellent saying of Gregory, "Let but a man get the love of the world in his heart, and he will quickly be rich." So if you will but get the love of religion in your heart, you will quickly be rich in grace. Love is a vigorous, active grace. It despises dangers, it tramples upon difficulties. Like a mighty torrent, it carries all before it. This is the grace which takes heaven by violence. Get but your hearts well heated with this grace and you will be fitted for work.

A third thing conducive to salvation is to work in the strength of Christ. *"I can do all things through Christ that strengthens me,"* Phil.3:13. Never go to work alone. Sampson's strength lay in his hair, and a Christian's strength lies in Christ. When you are to do any duty, to resist any temptation, to subdue any lust, set upon it in the strength of Christ. Some go out to fight sin in the strength of resolutions and vows. They are soon foiled. Do as Sampson. He first cried to

The One Thing Necessary

heaven for help, and then, having taken hold of the pillars, pulled down the house upon the lords of the Philistines. When we engage Christ in the work, and so take hold upon the pillar of an ordinance, we then bring down the house upon the head of our lusts.

Fourthly, work low, be humble, do not think that you will merit anything by your working. Either Satan will keep us from working or else he will make us proud of our working. God must pardon our works before He crowns them. If we could pray as angels, shed rivers of tears, build churches, erect hospitals, and should have a conceit that we merited anything by this, it would be as a dead fly in the box of perfume. It would stain and eclipse the glory of the work. Our duties, like good wine, taste of a bad cask. They are but glittering sins. Let not pride poison our holy things. When we have been working for heaven, we should say as did good Nehemiah, *"Remember me, O my God, concerning this, and spare me according to the greatness of Thy mercy,"* Neh.13:22.

Fifthly, work upon your knees, be much in prayer. Beg the Spirit of God to help you in the work. Make that prayer, *"Awake, O north wind, and come thou south, blow upon my garden,"* Canticles 4. We need to have this spirit blow upon us, there being so many contrary winds blowing against us, and considering how soon holy affections are apt to wither. The garden does not need more wind to make its fruit flow than

The One Thing Necessary

we need of the Spirit to make our graces flourish.

Phillip joined himself to the eunuch's chariot, God's Spirit must join itself to our chariot. As the mariner has his hand to the stern, so he has his eyes to the stars. While we are working, we must look up to the Spirit. What is our preparation without the Spirit's operation? What is all our rowing without a gale from heaven? *"The Spirit lifted me up,"* Ezek.3:14. God's Spirit must both infuse grace and excite it. We read of a wheel within a wheel, Ezek.1:16. The Spirit of God is that inner wheel that must move the wheel of our endeavors. To conclude all, pray to God to bless you in your work. *"The race is not to the swift, nor the battle to the strong,"* Ecc.9:1. Nothing prospers without a blessing, and what way to obtain it but by prayer? It is a saying of one of the Ancients, " The saints carry the keys of heaven at their girdle." Prayer beats the weapon out of the enemy's hands and gets the blessing out of God's hand.

Lastly, work in hope. The Apostle said, *"he that plows shall plow in hope,"* I Cor.9:10. Hope is the soul's anchor, Heb.6:19. Cast this anchor upon the promise and you shall never sink. Nothing more hinders us in our working than unbelief. "Sure," said a Christian, "I may toil all the day and catch nothing." What? Is there no balm in Gilead? Is there no mercy seat? Oh, sprinkle faith in every duty, look up to free grace, fix your eye upon the blood of Christ. Would

The One Thing Necessary

you be saved? To your working, join believing.

FINIS